D0396892

Also by Charles McGrath

AS EDITOR

Donald Barthelme: Collected Stories

John O'Hara: Stories

Golf Stories

The Summer Friend

The Summer Friend

A MEMOIR

Charles McGrath

Alfred A. Knopf
New York
2022

THIS IS A BORZOI BOOK
PUBLISHED BY ALFRED A. KNOPF

Copyright © 2022 by Charles A. McGrath

All rights reserved. Published in the United States by Alfred A. Knopf,
a division of Penguin Random House LLC, New York, and distributed
in Canada by Penguin Random House Canada Limited, Toronto.

www.aaknopf.com

Knopf, Borzoi Books, and the colophon are registered
trademarks of Penguin Random House LLC.

Library of Congress Cataloging-in-Publication Data
Names: McGrath, Charles, author.
Title: The summer friend : a memoir / Charles McGrath.
Description: First edition. | New York : Alfred A. Knopf, 2022. |
"This is a Borzoi Book"
Identifiers: LCCN 2021038975 (print) | LCCN 2021038976 (ebook) |
ISBN 9780593321157 (hardcover) | ISBN 9780593321164 (ebook)
Subjects: LCSH: McGrath, Charles—Childhood and youth. |
Journalists—United States—Biography. | Editors—United States—
Biography. | New England—Biography. | LCGFT: Autobiographies.
Classification: LCC PN4874.M483974 A3 2022 (print) |
LCC PN4874.M483974 (ebook) |
DDC 818/.609 [B]—dc23/eng/20211206
LC record available at https://lccn.loc.gov/2021038975
LC ebook record available at https://lccn.loc.gov/2021038976

Jacket photograph by Henk Meijer / Alamy
Jacket design by Chip Kidd

Manufactured in the United States of America
First Edition

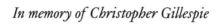

In memory of Christopher Gillespie

The Summer Friend

Getting Started

When I was growing up my family spent every July or August in a homemade summer house—little more than a shack, really. But the weeks we spent there seemed special to me back then—enchanted almost—and the spell has not entirely worn off. I still love summer and look forward to it like a kid awaiting the end of school. Summer is when I've had the most fun in my life—swimming, sailing, golfing, just goofing off. Summer is when I fell in love with the woman I married. And summer is when I was lucky enough to enjoy a long and unusual friendship at a time when I thought I was past making new friends. My friend has been dead for seven years now, but I still find it hard to think about summer without also thinking about him. It's not as if he left a hole, exactly. I still do many of the same things we used to do together, and I no longer actively mourn him. But he's an indelible part of many recollections, and I find it sweetly, if sadly, pleasurable sometimes to play them over in my head. Whenever I try to tell my own summertime story, I find myself telling a story that is partly his.

He was called Chip, and so to start with, we shared a name. I've been known as Chip most of my life, except for a brief period in college when I tried to reinvent myself as Charlie. This Chip and I both had five-year-old sons named Ben—not majorly weird, but a little—and eight-year-old daughters. In most other respects we couldn't have been more different. He was five years older and had grown up near Phillips Exeter Academy, in New Hampshire, where his father taught classics and briefly was headmaster. I grew up in a two-family house in Brighton, one of Boston's working-class neighborhoods. He was a WASP; I was Irish Catholic. He was a Vietnam vet (Coast Guard, with service on the Mekong Delta) who opposed the war but loved the military. I was a draft dodger who hated taking orders from anyone.

We met in August 1982, at a square dance, of all places. There were square dances every Saturday at the Methodist church in the little Massachusetts town where for a couple of summers my wife, Nancy, and I had been renting a house overlooking a tidal river. We didn't know anyone there. It was just us—Nancy, me, and the kids—enjoying an old-fashioned sort of summer: no TV, no phone calls, our only entertainments books, the beach, the river, occasional trips to the ice cream place. Somehow, though, we heard about the square dance and gathered that for a lot of people it was the high point of the week. Not me. I thought square-dancing was corny. I was also terrible at it, always turning the wrong way, and I have memories of being steered around like a floor lamp by a stern, impatient woman who turned out to be one of Chip's aunts. We went mostly for the sake of the kids, thinking this might be a place for them to make summer friends, and that's what happened—to them and to us. Ben joined a bunch of little boys in khaki shorts and polo shirts, all of them trying not to look too goofily self-conscious. Our daughter, Sarah, who loved any kind of dancing, joined a circle of little girls in summer dresses, their hair washed and braided, and quickly learned from them how to allemande and promenade. And Nancy and I met Chip and his wife, Gay. They were both, I couldn't help noticing, exceptionally good square dancers. They even knew how to do the Black Nag, a country dance so insanely complicated it made me dizzy just to watch.

We talked for a bit, the four of us. The conversation was friendly enough—the kids, the weather, the

upcoming school year—but if anything, only empha-
sized our differences. We were renters in town, they
were year-round and, unlike us, knew practically all
the people in the room. They were apparently related
to half of them. Then, out of the blue, Gay invited us
for supper the next night. She was always doing that,
we found out. She was an excellent cook and loved
having people around. He seemed shyer, but even so,
to welcome the idea.

It turned out they lived on the other side of the
river from where we were staying, just off the town's
main road, in a house almost hidden by tall bushes in
front. We missed it on the first pass and had to back up
before pulling into the driveway, almost scraping a big
post of vine-covered granite on the right. The house
was a remodeled Cape, gray with dark green shutters,
to which Chip had added a lookout tower, pretty much
just for the hell of it. The first thing I remember seeing, in the entrance hall, was an upright piano with an
enormous model of a whaling ship on top.

Though it was summer, we ate indoors at the dining room table, overlooked by a gilt-framed portrait of
some nineteenth-century gent with astonishing side-
whiskers. Bushrod Somebody-or-Other, one of Chip's
ancestors. We talked some more, the way couples do
when fishing for clues about each other: where you're

from, where you went to school, what you do for a living. We learned that Chip was an architect and that Gay was a stay-at-home mom who ran a flower business on the side. The flowers all grew out back, in a huge garden, along with their own vegetables. She took gardening very seriously, it became clear, and worked hard at it. Ten years younger than Chip, she had dropped out of college to marry him. I remember thinking she seemed almost hippieish, with long hair, almost to her waist, and wearing an ankle-length skirt and a peasant blouse. I thought he seemed like a grown-up—certainly more of one than I was. He had sandy hair, a broad forehead, and a wry expression, and once I learned he was of Scottish heritage—something he took immense pride in—I decided he looked a little like portraits of James Boswell, the great Samuel Johnson biographer.

For a time they had lived in Seattle, Gay explained, while Chip finished architecture school, and they had even thought of settling there, but they came back east—in a psychedelic Volkswagen bus—because they wanted to raise a family in the town where they had both spent their summers. They were like a couple in a New England lifestyle magazine, I thought, an advertisement for a new kind of homesteading.

A few days later, we had them back. (Their four-month-old, Kate, arrived in a basket.) While Nancy fixed some side dishes in the kitchen, I grilled swordfish on a little hibachi I had set on the wide porch railing of our rented house. It burned a big dent in the wood underneath, and I spent hours later with sandpaper trying to erase the evidence. Chip noticed the mess, I'm pretty sure, but didn't say anything. That was typical of him. He was seldom critical and had a gift for overlooking things when he wanted to.

Most of my friends then were people like me—writers or editors or people in book publishing. What I initially liked about Chip was that he was none of those things. One of the reasons we were renting a house in that town, and not in the Hamptons, say, or just across the bay on Martha's Vineyard, was that I wanted a break from the hothouse of New York publishing. I loved that there were no writers to meet, no literary cocktail parties to attend. I probably appealed to Chip for the opposite reason: I was someone he could talk about books with. He was actually less of a reader than he would have had you believe, but he loved the idea of books—loved having them around—and he also liked hearing stories about the people who wrote them.

It also turned out that, for all our differences, Chip and I had shared a common New England boyhood. Sports, for one thing—hockey especially, which we had learned to play not in rinks but on frozen ponds. And the Red Sox, of course. Following them was practically a civic religion in New England back then, one that imparted, or so we were taught, the ennobling lessons of failure. We had also watched the same children's TV shows. There weren't many in those days, and they were all pretty dreary, especially one called *Small Fry Club,* whose host was a creepy, ukulele-playing white-haired guy known as "Big Brother" Bob Emery. (I guess neither he nor his producers read much Orwell.) Chip astonished me that evening by remembering every word of Big Brother's theme song:

The grass is always greener
in the other fellow's yard.
The little row we have to hoe,
Oh boy that's hard.
But if we all could wear
green glasses now,
it wouldn't be so hard
to see how green the grass is
in our own backyard.

He didn't just recite it—he sang the whole thing, something I would never have dared in front of people I barely knew.

Still, after those first two evenings I can't say that I knew Chip very well. Nancy and I just agreed that we liked him and Gay and felt lucky to have found a family with a girl almost exactly Sarah's age and a boy Ben's. What really began our friendship—for me, anyway—was an afternoon a few days after that swordfish dinner when Sarah had a playdate with Alison, Chip and Gay's daughter. Gay dropped Alison off in their Dodge Caravan, but when it was time for her to be picked up, Chip arrived in a sailboat. We had learned by then that his ancestral homestead—the summer place his grandparents had built back at the turn of the twentieth century—was right across the water from us. It was high up on a hill—the shore on the other side was much steeper—and almost hidden by trees. From the house we were renting, you could just make out the hint of a roofline. At the foot of the hill was a dock and an anchorage where his extended clan moored their boats. They were all keen sailors, and here came probably the best of them tacking smartly through a squiggly channel in the marsh. I hadn't known it was possible to get from one side to the other like that. It was low tide, just marsh grass and mudflats, but Chip swooped through effortlessly. Coming near to our side, he stood up, pulled quickly on the sheet, and then ducked as the boom snapped around from one side of the boat to the other. A jibe like that is easily the trickiest maneuver in sailing, one fraught with opportunities for embarrassment, if not outright catastrophe—and this was as handsome as any I had ever seen. The boat glided to a stop, sail fluttering, and Alison waded out and climbed aboard. She was in her bathing suit, and when they got out into deeper water, Chip tossed out a line and Alison jumped overboard and grabbed it. While we watched from shore, he started towing her home.

Who knew you could do that with a sailboat, and how could you not want to be friends with the guy who thought of it?

Summer: A Short History

What we think of as summertime is really a human invention. In this country, the idea of vacations—of taking time off from work, going somewhere to get out of the heat—didn't come along until the nineteenth century, and it was initially embraced by people who didn't work all that hard to begin with. It was the rich who, especially during the Gilded Age, began to ritualize summer, traveling by steamer or train to the resort hotels, those huge wooden layer cakes, that began sprouting all up and down the East Coast. And it was the rich—or the super-rich, really—who started building summer places of their own: "camps" in the Adirondacks, twenty-thousand-square-foot "cottages" on the cliffs in Newport. Working people didn't get time off, and farmers, in particular, were busiest during the hot summer months. Schools let children out during the summer not so they could be idle, or because the teacher needed a break, but so they could help in the fields.

Summer didn't have to be idle. Some early camping spots, like Oak Bluffs, on Martha's Vineyard, or Ocean Grove, in New Jersey, had a religious component; others, most notably Chautauqua, in western New York, were founded on the idea of self-improvement, both moral and physical. But the great resorts had about them an air of exclusivity: you went there to be among people like yourself. What exactly people did at these places is—to me, anyway—a bit of a mystery. Swimming was not an especially popular activity in the late nineteenth century, especially for women, who had to wear bathing costumes so cumbersome and concealing that, when wet, they practically dragged the swimmer under. There would have been sailing, and golf of course. Around 1890 golfing became a kind of national craze among the well-to-do in America, and country clubs sprang up everywhere. I'm also guessing that then, as now, there was more sex in summer than in the rest of the year. But in the novels of the period—I'm thinking of Henry James and Edith Wharton—there's scarcely any mention of such activities. What people mostly did was stroll around and wait for the next meal, sort of like people in rest homes: breakfast, luncheon, tea, dinner. They also changed clothes a lot and gossiped incessantly about each other. Some of those grand old resorts still exist, and to visit one—Pinehurst, say, in North Carolina, or The Balsams in New Hampshire—is a little like visiting an old cathedral, a monument to an ancient belief system. They all have long verandas, for strolling, snoozing, or cigar-smoking, and enormous dining rooms—the chapels, so to speak. A string quartet might drone away at one end, or a piano player tinkle out something inoffensive, while squads of uniformed waiters carried in course after course: terrapin, canvasbacks, salmon, turbot, roasts of veal and beef, followed by the jellies and aspics so popular then. Plenty of wine if you wanted it, and surely many did: they must have been bored silly.

A lot of things hastened the decline of this summer-resort culture, not least its own wasteful extravagance. But what pretty much ended it for good—except for a few grand holdouts, which now seem like nineteenth-century theme parks—was the advent of the automobile, which enabled people to go where they wanted, not where the railroads took them, and, especially after the war, allowed middle-class families to enjoy summer spaces of their own. Instead of the great verandaed hotel there was the motor court, a little cluster of cabins by the highway, and, increasingly, the family place, the seaside cottage, the little cabin on the lake. For two weeks or a month every year they offered families, children and grown-ups alike, a uniquely American kind of escape, a chance to reinvent yourself: to go barefoot, look up at the stars, read the books you always hoped to, and become the person—freer, easier, tanner, thinner—you were always meant to be.

If you're like me, summer memories pile up in no particular order. Endless car trips, your thighs sticking to the pale green vinyl of the back seat, where your brother has crossed the invisible halfway boundary and now, despite your father's shout, "Cut it out, you two," requires a firm disciplinary kick to the shin. Ball games and barbecues, fireworks and fireflies. Also mosquito bites, poison ivy, and sometimes—if your ice cream man was as irresponsible as ours, letting his wares thaw and refreeze—ptomaine poisoning. One summer I threw up twenty-seven times in a row. And let's not forget about sunburn. Back before anyone knew about skin cancer, you could fry yourself senseless in the midday glare and then stagger indoors, lobster-red and so hot you felt shivery. At night the touch of a sheet on your bare back was almost unendurable. But then, in a couple of days, you got to peel the skin from your shoulders, long strips lifting up like wax paper from a roll—a process so satisfying it was like sloughing off your own cocoon.

For a lot of people summer is connected to a particular place. That mothball-smelling rental cottage your family took every year for the last two weeks of July, the one with holes in the screens, flypaper in the kitchen, creepy-looking stains on the blue-ticked mattresses. Your old summer camp, the one with color wars, campfire ghost stories, and the teenage counselors, godlike in their wisdom and experience, who taught you how to short-sheet the beds of the new kids. (I went to summer camp for just one week when I was eleven and hated every minute, but I'm probably the exception. It didn't help that the place my parents picked was Catholic, on the grounds of an old seminary, and that we spent almost as much time on our knees in the chapel as we did in the crumbling concrete pool.) Or the summer place you remember best could be your grandparents' house, where they doted on you like royalty and where you got to sleep alone in a room—no sibling for a change!—with the windows open and the white cotton curtains stirring in the evening breeze.

Summer can happen almost anywhere. You could be blissful in the rear seat of the station wagon, where you dozed contentedly, or looked out the window and played punch buggy with your sister, while on the annual trip to a national park. You could feel preposterously alive and happy at the tarmac playground where you went every summer morning and played box hockey while the little kids, shrieking, danced around in the sprinkler. If worse came to worst that special summer place could even be your own room, transformed for eight weeks or so into a sanctuary of unimaginable freedom: no homework, no bedtime, no getting out of pajamas all day if you didn't feel like it.

For Chip that special place was the house where his mother and his grandparents had spent their summers—the place on the hill across from us. It was called Snowdon—Snowdie for short—after the mountain in Wales so beloved by Wordsworth and the other Romantics. It was a two-story shingle-style building at the top of a steep slope leading down to the water. There was a big, unkempt lawn in front, and a long, narrow porch in back. Built in 1902, the place was once fairly grand—a relic from that era when summer belonged mostly to the well-to-do—but to keep it up had become a bit of a struggle. Chip cherished it all the same—the house and all its summer history. That was one of the first things that struck me about him—that he chose to live year-round in what was for many people just a summer town, and had made summering into something like an occupation.

The Camp

When I was a boy we used to spend our summers, or half of them, at a place we called the Camp. We'd go there in July one year, August the next—except for the magical year of 1956, when because of the polio epidemic we didn't go back to school and lingered there until October. Years later I met someone—he was the father of one of our daughter's first boyfriends—who also went to a place he called the Camp, and it too was in Massachusetts, and it too was ramshackle and cobbled together and had only rudimentary plumbing. I think now there must have been Camps everywhere—do-it-yourself summer places—but none could have been better or more important than ours. It was at the Camp that I learned how to be a summer person. My love of boats was kindled there, and so, after a fashion, was my love of golf. At the Camp, I first got an inkling of what grown-up summers might be like—the sex part especially. And it was at the Camp that I discovered the thrill of lawlessness and rule-breaking, an ongoing theme in summers to come.

My companion in those days was my brother Tom, two years younger—my original summer friend, you could say. If Chip reminded me of someone I had played with as a child, Tom was the genuine article, someone I played with practically from the moment he was born. He had the additional virtue of being infinitely obliging, game for anything I suggested, and in mischief even more advanced than I was. It was Tom, for example, who one summer dared to insert a cigarette load into one of our mother's Old Golds. Cigarette loads were tiny bits of explosive, and, hard to believe now, you could buy them at a joke shop. You stuck one—a little wooden sliver, like a matchstick—into the tobacco end of a cigarette and when the smoker lit up, it would go off with a loud bang and blow the cigarette apart. Childish, I know, but the memory of my mother standing there, wide-eyed, with an exploded cigarette in her mouth still makes me tear up with laughter.

Tom was also precocious about drinking and got us started early, when we were barely into our teens. Beer, it turned out, produced a much more satisfactory buzz than the model-airplane glue I had us experimenting with. I can't say that we got into trouble only at the Camp. At home over the years we had so many misadventures—some alcohol-related, some just stupid—that we were practically on a first-name basis with the staff at the local emergency room. All the same, there was something about the Camp that encouraged daring and recklessness.

Originally the Camp had been just that: a campsite, with a tent, on some thinly wooded land near Nabnasset Lake, in Westford, Massachusetts. (Strictly speaking, the lake was really a pond, but no one ever called it that. It seemed too big to be a pond. There was a swamp at one end and a public beach at the other, half a mile away. We were on the poor, hilly side. Across the way were summer houses with lawns stretching down to the water and docks where speedboats were tied up. That's where the doctors lived, or so we were told.) Sometime before the war, my grandfather, my father, and his younger brother built a one-room cabin on the site. Later, they added on to that a kitchen and dining area. Still later they put up another cabin— a living room with a brick fireplace and built-in corner bunks—and eventually they connected this cabin to the other with a roofed-over, walled-in breezeway. Not long after that, they stuck onto the breezeway a bathroom and two bedrooms, made of shiny yellowish wallboard that reminded me of flypaper that had lost its stickiness.

In the kitchen, the stove, the sink, and the refrigerator were all on different levels. The living room, because it had once been a separate building, had double barn doors and windows that looked onto the breezeway. The whole place had a haphazard, accidental quality, and to a child that was part of its appeal. Just by the way it looked and the way it smelled— a little damp and a little musty—the Camp announced itself as a place where the normal conventions did not apply. You wore shorts and T-shirts, and went without shoes. Most of our meals were at a picnic table, and to save dishwashing we often ate off paper plates. There must have been rules about bedtime, but I don't remember any. I remember going to bed and getting up when I felt like it, and it seems to me now that I didn't sleep very much at all. I lazed in bed while my brother, in the bunk below me, practiced farting. The bunks were Navy surplus—racks, made of thick, gray-painted boards—and could withstand any amount of jumping, something not tolerated at home. From mine, on top, you could reach up and dangle from the rafters or else swing over the wall, which did not reach the ceiling, and drop down into the room next door, bouncing on the bed there. Officially this was my parents' room, but so what? At the Camp you could do whatever you wanted.

The land the Camp occupied had been won by my grandfather in a raffle at something called the Sportsmen's Show, or that was the family myth, and it seemed fitting. To my brother and me, and to my father, too, the Camp was a windfall, one of the luckiest things ever to happen to a family otherwise not especially fortunate. Every winter, my father made a point of taking us to the Sportsmen's Show, a hunting, camping, and fishing exhibition held at the Mechanics Building in downtown Boston. We were not a hunting, camping, or fishing family. We never did any of those things. We were a boating family—at least aspirationally—and the Sportsmen's Show had no boats that I recall except canoes. There was a big water tank where fly fishermen put on exhibitions. Ted Williams did some casting there one year. There was also a stage where, another year, Jack Sharkey, a retired prizefighter, boxed with a kangaroo. Sharkey, I remember, came out in a robe and trunks, as if for a real bout. The kangaroo, wearing boxing gloves on its front legs, leaned back on its tail and made some feeble pawing motions while Jack danced around him. The ref declared it a draw.

I think now that our trips to that show may have been for my father a kind of rite—a way of commemorating the good fortune that brought the Camp into the family, and of remembering earlier summers there, especially the ones when he, his father, and his brother were building the place. He didn't talk very much, especially about himself, but I suspect those early summers were a sort of charmed time for him. For one thing, my father's mother, to whom he was particularly close, was still alive then and she would have been looking out for him.

My father was a disappointment to the rest of his family. The favorite was his younger brother, Tom, or else his sister, JoAnn, whom everyone doted on. Tom was smarter and better-looking and didn't stammer the way my father sometimes did, and my grandfather decided that when it came to education Tom was by far the surer bet. My father, Charlie (for whom I am named), was dreamy—slow, my grandfather thought—and more interested in mechanical things than in books. He didn't get into Latin School, Boston's elite high school, and went instead to Boston English, for lesser young men, the ones without classical fineness, and eventually flunked out. Tom went to Latin and excelled, and afterward my grandfather paid for him not just to attend but to live at MIT, when he could easily have commuted from the family home in Brighton. My father was left to fend for himself, and went for a while to Wentworth Institute, a technical school, but never finished. Amazingly, he never resented his brother. He admired Tom, just as everyone else did, and was devastated when Tom died in the war while piloting a fighter in the South Pacific. Whenever the World War II movie *The Fighting Lady* was shown on TV, our whole family made a point of watching it, because if you looked closely, or so my father said, you could catch a glimpse of Uncle Tom. My guess is that the summer of 1941, when they were at the Camp, was probably the last extended time they spent together, and I think that may have accounted for my father's general unwillingness to change very much about the place.

My grandfather was known as Mac, and my brother and I despised him. He was a cranky, humorless old man, who showed up at the Camp every summer and made everyone miserable. He was a retired postmaster, who wore three-piece suits and expected deference. He also had something wrong with his feet, which had to be soaked in Epsom salts and then wrapped, just so, in Ace bandages. This was my mother's job. She'd bring the tub of hot water and then kneel like a handmaiden, winding the bandages while Mac yelled, "More slack! More slack!"

What's scary is that every now and then I catch a glimpse of Mac in the mirror. Mac is me! The same jowls, the same cleft in the chin that gets deeper and deeper every year, a little cavern sprouting whiskers impossible to shave. As I get older I look more and more like him, and I am now, God help me, probably approaching the exact age he was then. I worry that I have also inherited some of his personality. I am not cranky, or not usually, but I used to have a temper, and I detect in myself sometimes Mac's flintiness—his meanness of spirit. Though I didn't think so for most of my adolescence and young manhood, the person I now wish I were more like is my father. He had a gentleness and a sweetness about him that I foolishly mistook for dullness. He died much too soon, at fifty-nine, much younger than I am now, and before we could get over being disappointments to each other.

In my mind's eye I keep a black-and-white photograph of my father and me standing in the lake at the Camp. He is tall and slender, his hair is swept back, and, because he has been swimming, he is not wearing his glasses. His eyes are serious and thoughtful. I must be five or six and don't come to much above his waist, so scrawny that my skin seems too tightly stretched over my bones. I look like a plucked bird. But my eyes are gleaming with pleasure. My father seldom swam with us. He would take a quick dip in the evening, in lieu of a shower, but mostly the lake was for our enjoyment and not his. So this must have been some special occasion. My birthday maybe? Why else would anyone take a picture? If there were summer moments you could go back and retrieve, that one would be high on my list.

My mother loathed the Camp. This was partly snobbishness. She thought of herself as a seashore person, a higher calling, and also looked down on our neighbors, not all of whom were summer people. Some were living by the lake not for recreation but just because land out there was cheap. But my mother also had legitimate complaints. There was Mac, for example, and it was she, not my father, who wound up doing most of the caretaking. And often the hot water would go on the blink. If you needed some, you had to heat it on the stove. Laundry you did—or rather, my mother did—at the Laundromat in a nearby town. Bathing you did in the lake, with a bar of Ivory soap.

Sometimes there was no water at all. It was practically a yearly ritual that when we opened the Camp for the season my father would turn on the pump and nothing would happen. The pump was in a skunky-smelling cement-block chamber underneath the breezeway. To reach it you had to move a wicker settee, roll up a woven rug, and open a trapdoor in the floor. The pump, which ran off a belt from a small electric motor, had a big red flywheel and looked like something from an old-fashioned fire truck. There must have been some kind of collection tank down there, but I can't picture it. The pump hole, as we called it, was dark, damp, a little scary, and when I was young I didn't like to look down there very much. What I mostly remember is that my father, wearing a sleeveless undershirt and carrying a trouble light on an extension cord, would descend for what seemed like days, having his meals and the occasional can of beer handed down to him, while he tried to get the pump running again. My father was shy and soft-spoken, and almost never swore, but from down in the pump hole you would hear mutterings like "Gol darn it!" and "Hell's bells!"

The solution would have been a new pump, of course. The family who lived across the road had recently installed something called a jet pump, which instead of a fire engine resembled a torpedo, and from them you got the impression that their water pressure was so strong it would knock you over. But we didn't have the money, and even if we had, it would not have mattered. My father preferred to patch and fix things rather than replace them, and long before it was fashionable he was a committed recycler. When I was in graduate school, he built a desk for me partly out of old hockey sticks. It had only two legs instead of four, because he didn't want to waste the lumber, and getting it to balance was a little like erecting a house of cards.

No water at the Camp meant takeout for supper. The whole time I was growing up, we never once had pizza or Chinese food, and I'm not sure such exotic dishes were even available in Westford, Massachusetts, in the mid-fifties. My mother would drive my brother and me to a roadhouse we called Polly's Plane, because there was a real plane on the roof—of the same kind my father's brother used to fly, I liked to imagine—and order spaghetti and meatballs to go. There were probably closer, better places for takeout, but my mother was fond of her cocktails, and at Polly's she could enjoy a couple of Manhattans while waiting for the spaghetti to be cooked and then packed into round cardboard containers, where invariably it congealed and turned waxy before we got home. If my mother had time for another Manhattan before my father emerged from the pump hole, she would then berate him for not providing us all with a more suitable summer place. Her sister Libby, she would remind us all, had a place on the ocean.

Social class and my father's insufficiency as a provider were ongoing themes in my parents' marriage. They met under false pretenses, at a UFO dance for officers only. My father, an enlisted man, had borrowed a lieutenant's uniform after hearing that a nicer kind of girl went to the officers' dances. He spotted my mother and fell in love, and they wound up marrying, but in some ways, she never forgave him for not being a lieutenant.

At home, in Brighton, we lived on the first floor of a two-family house, the same house my father was born in. This was another sore point with my mother, who felt that she deserved a house of her own, and that my father had been bullied into taking over the two-family, so that Mac, who had built it, could move down the street to a nicer, single house, where he lived with my father's sister and her family. One more sore point on an ever-growing list of them: Mac, or so we were taught to believe, supported that family while JoAnn's husband, Uncle Dick (who had been an officer during the war, and not a mere enlisted man), got both law and business degrees. So there was always an air of disappointment and confinement around the Brighton house. We had a yard but it felt small and hemmed-in, and for some reason, despite all my father's efforts, grass refused to grow there. As often as not we played in the street.

The Camp, though far smaller than the Brighton house, felt by comparison large and full of possibility. When we packed up the car—a Studebaker in the early years, and then a green Chevy—heading west for the summer, even my mother was happy to get away. She would lean back in her seat, light up one of her Old Golds, and take a big drag of contentment. We had the whole summer stretching out ahead of us. And, for the moment, a cloudless blue horizon.

To get to Westford from Brighton back then you followed Route 2, through the towns of Watertown, Arlington, and Belmont, then headed north through Lexington and Concord, past the Concord Reformatory, where my parents would threaten to drop us off if we didn't behave, and through Bedford and Chelmsford, semirural then but now McMansioned bedroom communities. The ride took only an hour or so but seemed longer. Just beyond Chelmsford, you turned off onto Pine Road, a dirt lane, a little washed out at the bottom, lined with the pine trees. (At this point, I would crank down the car window for a big gulp of fresh air and pine smell, imagining we had entered the forest.) Then, up the hill, you made a right and at the top stood our Camp, red, board-sided, with a chimney at one end. Unlike the Brighton house, which was functional and unlovely, the Camp looked to me like a storybook house.

In my recollection, it only rained once at the Camp and then it poured for a week, and the yard, which was packed dirt because there was not enough sun to grow a lawn, became covered in puddles that grew into lakes. Bored silly, Tom and I stayed inside and played cards and Monopoly, which I always won because I persuaded him every time to accept a deal whereby I could have the railroads and he would get the utilities. We made a point of savoring the Fannie Farmer lollipops presented to us every summer, in a fancy box with a hollowed-out niche for each pop, by a kindly, white-haired lady named May Mullen, who was the girlfriend of Uncle Charlie, Mac's younger brother. May was single and lived in an apartment on Commonwealth Avenue. Did she have a job? How did she and Charlie meet? I have no idea. The only other thing I know about May Mullen is that she was murdered a few years later by Albert DeSalvo—the Boston Strangler, as the tabloids called him, a serial killer who preyed on women who lived alone. Or, rather, the autopsy suggested she died of fright just as Albert got his hands on her. She was so open and trusting I'm sure he talked his way in with no trouble at all.

Uncle Charlie too had been a postmaster and also wore three-piece suits, though not at the Camp. There, he wore a threadbare open-necked white shirt and a straw fedora. He drove a black Buick so polished it looked like an undertaker's car. Charlie was a bachelor. Back home in Brighton, he lived upstairs from us with his sister, whom we called Aunt Liza, and as far as I could make out—these things were never discussed—they couldn't stand each other. She would serve him his meals at the dining room table, where he sat at the end, his napkin tucked under his chin, while she ate by herself sitting on a wooden box in her room, which was at the front of the house, as far away from him as she could get. I never once heard them speak to each other, though in truth I didn't go up there much. Liza was scary and unfriendly, and the whole arrangement felt uncomfortably weird. Liza did not approve of May Mullen, and I suspect that Charlie and May's visits to the Camp were secret. It's interesting, now that I think of it, that they never came when Mac was visiting. Maybe the two brothers disliked each other—as I said, these things were never talked about—or maybe Mac also disapproved of May, which makes me wish now that I had known her better. All I remember is her twinkly blue eyes and the slightly grand, singsong voice in which, after looking us over, she would announce that my brother and I were "a fine pair of boys, yes, a fine pair of boys." I'd like to imagine that on the way home she and Charlie would stop at a motel—a tourist cabin, like the ones Lolita and Humbert Humbert stayed in—and get it on. But probably not. More likely he dropped her off at her apartment on Commonwealth Avenue and went back to Liza and her stony glances, and it may be that for him, too, the Camp was a temporary, sun-dappled idyll, a glimpse of another kind of life.

That rainy summer, the visits of Charlie and May were memorable because they were out of the ordinary. Most days at the camp were just like every other day. Predictability—reliability—was part of the appeal. But if you do the same things every year, one summer blends into the next. And the next. It's not a blur, exactly, but rather a long, arrested moment. Sometimes, I find myself connecting things that happened years apart. I went to the Camp starting when I was born, in 1947, and my last summer there was my fifteenth. But in my memories of the Camp, I'm mostly the same age, twelve or so. All those summers are one summer, one long, extended boyhood. And the self I recall is a different one from the self I was the rest of the time. At school I was bullied a bit because I was a goody-goody and a teacher's pet. But at the Camp I was popular, a leader among our little gang, some of them summer kids, some of them year-rounders. And I was a daredevil, not a bookworm. I was the kind of person who blasted tin cans in the woods with a borrowed .22 rifle my parents never knew about. To this day, the smell of gunpowder gives me a thrill, and I can pull back the slide and jack out that tiny brass cartridge in my sleep.

Back in Brighton, starting at the age of eight or nine, I became a reader. I would go to the library, take out five books, the most allowed, and a day or two later go back for five more. My father used to get angry when he asked me to help with one or another of his projects or inventions and I would arrive with my finger in a book. I must have read at the Camp—how could I not?—but I don't recall doing so, except on Sunday mornings, when I would spread the funnies out on the same rug that concealed the pump hole and read them there on the floor, my head propped up on my hands. My favorite time to read at home was in bed at night, but I can't now picture that there was even a light above my bunk at the Camp. In my memories I am always sweetly exhausted up there, a little sunburned and worn out by the day, hovering on the edge of sleep, too tired even to bother swatting the mosquito now buzzing around my head.

Tom and I left the house every morning, after breakfast at the picnic table, and were outside almost all day, with just a pit stop for lunch. What did we do to fill up all those hours? For one thing, we walked a lot. The small public beach down at the other end of the lake had a store, no bigger than a shed, that sold penny candy: licorice, red hots, little wax bottles filled with sweet, syrupy liquid. A trek there and back, under the hot sun with the cicadas buzzing, could eat up much of a morning. Halfway back you'd stop, bite off the top of one of those waxy little bottles, letting the syrup trickle down your throat, imagining that it was slaking your thirst. We hiked in the woods and once came upon a nest made by a tramp: a hollow of leaves and pine branches, in which he had left behind some empty whiskey pints and, thrillingly, a cache of nudie magazines. These weren't *Playboy*s, but smaller, cheesier magazines with grainy black-and-white photographs that seemed even dirtier than the full-color variety. I knew about breasts, but the revelation here was pubic hair, great, beard-like thatches of it. Who knew? I didn't act on it for years, but I felt then a stirring intimation that summer might also be a sexy season.

We swam, if you could call it that. There was a dock at our end of the lake and we jumped off it over and over, hour after hour. Cannonballs, kneedrops, the jump where you pretend you're Wile E. Coyote and scissor your legs in midair. Then, one summer, there were masks and swim fins and we went skin-diving, or that's what we said we were doing. We dove for what we called freshwater clams—mussels, I now realize—and came up with dripping handfuls. They were of no use whatsoever, but that didn't make them seem any less valuable until, at the end of the day, we tossed them all back.

We cooked out, or my parents did. The whole notion of cooking outdoors was just catching on then, or maybe it was just catching on with our family, and we never entirely got the hang of it. My father seemed to think it was flames, not coals, that supplied the best heat and put the steaks on way too soon, after first goosing the fire with an extra squirt of lighter fluid and causing a smoky orange flare-up. The meat always tasted faintly of kerosene.

We were bored some of the time, but children then were used to being bored, and summer boredom, sweet and listless, was its own reward. There was nothing to do, but there was nothing you were supposed to do. Time passed with syrupy slowness, and yet—this is one of the paradoxes of summer—the days at the Camp were also racing to an end and before you knew it, it was time to pack the car and head home. *Where did the summer go?* my mother sometimes said, lighting up another cig. Good question.

For most of my years there we split the summers with my aunt's family, who were not as attached to the place. In 1959, my father bought her share. She had more money and ought to have given it to him, or so my mother thought. We didn't know it, but that was really the beginning of the end. Four years later my father did the unthinkable and sold the place. There were money troubles. There were summer jobs: my brother and I had reached an age when we were expected to have them, and there were none to be found in Westford. And possibly my mother's dislike of the place finally wore my father down. My brother and I wept and pleaded when we heard the news, but suddenly, with the unexpected swiftness of a summer thunderstorm—the kind that whips up from nowhere and turns the sky dark as dusk—the Camp was no longer part of our lives.

And then the storm passed, the way summer storms so quickly do. We grew up, my brother and I, and we discovered girls and rum, not just beer, and driving around in cars. The Camp seldom came up in conversation except to acknowledge that it would have been a great place to have a party. In our memory the place was huge and welcoming, and we pictured sleepovers accommodating dozens of teenagers, some of them dancing, some of them probably passed out under the trees or on the bunks in the living room. We could have gotten away with anything there because the place was so remote. Who would know or find out?

Years later, when our parents were dead and we were both married, with families of our own, my brother and I went back to have a look at the Camp. I felt like Alice in Wonderland tumbling backward through the hole. In my mind the Camp had become a huge, log-timbered Adirondack lodge, surrounded by sunlit pines. But either the place had shrunk or, such are the transforming powers of the childhood imagination, this is what it really was all along—a sort of shack, on a squarish lot surrounded by spindly trees. The new owners, year-rounders, had let it go a little—the place had a sad, tired look—but not so much that I didn't realize it had always been a bit shabby and ramshackle. No wonder my mother felt so superior! The Camp then didn't seem summery at all—it seemed depressing and autumnal.

Part of what made the Camp important to all of us—even to my mother—was that it was a toehold on specialness, a perch on the middle class, where we really had no business belonging. People like us didn't have summer places. None of our neighbors at home did. And yet there we were every July, packing the car, my brother and I saying goodbye to our friends, telling them we'd see them in the fall. We were off to our summer house!

The phrase was so magical we were almost embarrassed to say it. It must have broken my father to give the place up. I was so preoccupied with my own longings and imaginings that I didn't even notice that without a place to go to, we stopped having vacations. I have (or used to have; he died much too young) another brother, ten years younger than I am, and a sister, fifteen years younger—a separate family almost—and one of the many things distancing us is that they had little recollection of the Camp. They never knew our family at its best.

About a year before my father died, he and my mother and my sister, who was still a young teenager, moved to Scituate, Massachusetts, where my mother's sister Libby had her summer house. Scituate, a town

on Massachusetts Bay, had once been a summer col-
ony (sometimes referred to as the Irish Riviera) but
was quickly turning into a year-round bedroom community. My parents' new house was just a block from
the ocean, and as my mother never tired of pointing
out, you could hear the waves. She at last had her
wish—the shore!—and would go around snuffling in
deep, melodramatic gasps of what she called the sea
air. My parents moved in part because Boston real-
estate prices were tumbling, and they wanted to get
what they could for the old two-family before it was
too late. But my mother also saw this as an opportunity, a final victory of sorts, with saltwater triumphing
over fresh, and the Camp and the legacy of my father's
family forever diminished.

The Scituate house was open and breezy, much
less cramped than the old two-family, and my mother
hoped it would be a new start for both of them, a year-
round summer place. But she failed to anticipate how
hard it would be to make friends there, and she began
to drink too much and spend hours on the phone talking to the ones she had left behind. And the commute
to Boston, where my father still worked, was fairly
brutal, not nearly as quick as the real-estate agent had
advertised. It took a toll on him. Married by then, I
wasn't able to visit much, but my sense is that the Sci-

tuate place was a disappointment to them both and that they blamed each other for that. It was a place they couldn't get away from. Eighteen months after they moved there, my father died of a heart attack, and nine months after that my mother was killed in a car wreck. No chance, really, for them to make a new life for themselves.

Loving, Plus Some
Breaking and Entering

Chip began going out with Gay in the spring of 1971. He was just back from Vietnam and living in Cambridge. Gay was at Boston University, not very happily, and when she learned that Chip was driving down every weekend to the old summer place to see his mother, she asked if she could hitch a ride. (Her family had moved to town, from Colorado, a few years before.) At first she and Chip just drove together, making idle conversation, but gradually the connection deepened. Chip told me once that he worried at first about the age difference between them but then decided what the heck. He courted Gay all during that summer and in August they got engaged. Originally he wanted a June wedding, but that seemed too long to wait, and so they were married at the tail end of summer, over Columbus Day weekend.

People meet and fall in love at other times of year,

of course, but the arrival of summer seems to promise a fresh start, an opportunity to meet someone out of the ordinary. The weather is nice, the sun is out, even your skin, newly bared after a winter of smothering, seems to come alive. This was the plot of all those *Gidget* movies back when I was a teen: you go to the beach, meet someone, fall in love, and become a brand-new person. We knew those movies were sappy, but a lot of us went anyway, because we wanted to believe it could happen to us. And sometimes it did. The sun-baked warmth of a female back under your Coppertone-smeared fingers, her bathing suit top daringly untied—you never forget something like that. Or the breathless sweetness of a late-July make-out session, the car radio softly playing, and the window cracked open just enough to let in the breeze.

That was another good thing about summer: more time for hanging around with the opposite sex and more places to do it. My friends and I used to play a lot of miniature golf—the boys in pressed chinos, the girls in Bermudas and sleeveless blouses. We were all a little self-conscious, the boys showing off, the girls making fun of how bad they were, but somehow it was romantic all the same. And the drive-in! Remember drive-ins? There are still a few around, but they've become curiosities, relics from a bygone age, and my sense is that people go to them now the way English tourists visit old churches—to remind themselves that once there were people who thronged such places, and that what happened there was once profoundly important.

My friends and I tended to go by the carload—because admission was per vehicle, not per head—and, stopped at red lights on the way, we would perform what we called a fire drill. Everyone would get out, run around the car, and then—except for the driver—get back in a different place. (This was easier back then, when so many cars still had bench seats.) I also knew some guys who had fixed up an old hearse, which they parked sideways, so they and their dates could recline and watch the movie from the window that used to display the coffin. But the ideal way to go to the drive-in was as a twosome—just you and your date.

For me, like many boys in the fifties and sixties, the secrets of love and of the automobile were inextricably linked, and I was a little slow about both. Next door to us in Brighton there was a family of teenagers who were serious hot-rodders. In their garage, separated from ours by a scraggly grapevine, they and their friends souped up their own cars—including an enormous tomato-red '57 Caddy, as stately as a yacht, and a docile-seeming black '52 Ford that gave no hint of the dual carbs and twin headers that slept under the hood—and then moved on to building and racing stock cars. One of them even became an Indy driver.

That garage was to me a wizards' den, a cave of forbidden mysteries. When I was young I used to peer between the grape leaves while those young mechanics went about their tasks, welding, bolting, lifting engines out with a chain hoist, scooting under a jacked-up chassis on little dollies. As I got older and more daring I squeezed through the vine and began to hang out, hardly noticed, in a dark, oily-smelling corner. I watched and I listened. All of the boys were immensely gifted swearers, and from them I picked up a lot of vocabulary I use to this day. I learned even more when they talked about sex, which they did all the time, and not just theoretically. One of them had "knocked up" his girlfriend—his lingo—and was debating whether to marry her. Another announced one afternoon that he had performed oral sex on a girl—"ate her out"—and she had practically fainted. Until that moment I had not known that such an act was even possible, and I concluded that sex, like auto mechanics, must be largely a matter of know-how. You had to understand what went on under the hood.

My own expertise was pretty rudimentary. I was timid and uncertain to begin with, and because I went to an all-boys high school, my experience with girls was limited for a long time to sneaking glances at the Catholic schoolgirls, in their knee socks and short plaid uniform skirts, across the subway platform at the Park Street MTA station. And though I dreamed of having a car of my own and fixing it up, that was out of the question financially. When I began to go on dates I had to borrow my father's wheels. First there was a clunky 1960 Ford Galaxie with an expanse of gull-wing trunk that, while taking a girl to dinner after a dance at her school, I inadvertently backed into the lobby of a Chinese restaurant, bringing down a shower of plate glass. Then there was a snappier '63 Corvair with bucket seats and a weird toggle-like shift selector on the dashboard. This was the car that Ralph Nader famously called "unsafe at any speed," and for good reason. The back end had a tendency to slew sidewise, and I sometimes tried to make this happen, usually in the tunnel at the end of Storrow Drive in Boston. The poor girl next to me would squeal in terror, which I mistook for excitement and admiration.

The real point in those days was not driving but parking. My favorite spot was a reservoir not far from our house where on summer evenings dozens of cars would be nestled, nose in, against the verge and looking out over the rez, as we called it, shining darkly like a mirror. If you listened carefully, you might hear the tick, tick of the engine cooling under the hood, or a snatch of song—the Beatles or the Beach Boys—faintly from a car down the row. My first serious girlfriend was just as inexperienced as I but, to my surprise, liked parking as much as I did, and steadily we made the prescribed way from first base to second to third.

We never made it to home plate. I don't think either of us really wanted to get there—and so we often just sat and cuddled, breathing in the night air. I would go home dazed and sated, tasting lipstick on my mouth, and still smelling her hair from where it had been pressed against my cheek.

Parking, sadly, is on its way out. The police are more vigilant, for one thing, and if you believe the people who worry about the future of the automotive industry, teenagers are no longer besotted with cars and eager to get their licenses at the first opportunity. They ride in Ubers instead. And why make out in a car, especially one with a driveshaft hump or a center console, when you can do it at home? A friend of mine used to allow his thirteen-year-old son to entertain girlfriends in his bedroom with the door shut. It was a little awkward, he said, but then he shrugged, as if to say, "What can you do?" I know I would have

47

died rather than let my parents know what I was up to, especially my mother, who was fierce on the subject of chastity. Sex was too beautiful and holy even to talk about, she told us frequently, and only animals had it before marriage.

I began going out with Nancy in the summer of 1968, when we both found ourselves in New Haven. I had just graduated from Yale, where I had gone on scholarship. I was always smart, or, rather, good at school—not necessarily the same thing, as I have learned—and figured out early on that academic success would be my meal ticket. I worked hard—too hard, I now think, driven by ambition but also by a genuine love of the books I read. I determined then that somehow I would make my living in the literary world, though I had no idea how to go about it. Earlier that year I had won a fellowship to study in England, and now I was teaching in a summer program for grammar school kids. Nancy, equipped with a brand-new master's degree from the Yale Graduate School, was teaching summer school while waiting to begin a high school teaching job in the fall. We already knew each other a little, because the previous fall we had been in the same class together, an English seminar open only to senior boys (undergraduate Yale was all-male back then) and graduate-school women. The professor was a famous scholar named W. K. Wimsatt, who was almost seven feet tall, like a giant in a fairy tale. I think his idea was that some female presence might civilize us a little. Nancy was barely aware of me then, but I was certainly aware of her. She was brilliant and she was beautiful. But she chose not to take the second semester of the course, and the rest of the school year I saw her just once, when I went to see her act in a play. I don't remember very much about it, except that in one scene she wore a housedress and carried a mop. I think she was supposed to be elderly, but she was too youthful to carry it off.

That summer, we ran into each other late one afternoon and wound up having dinner together. A couple of days later we had dinner again, and soon we were having dinner together every night. It just happened. We never talked about it, or made formal plans—we just arranged to run into each other every evening around dinnertime.

On our first official date, we went frog-hunting in Edgewood Creek, something I had done a few days earlier with the kids I was teaching. In retrospect, it seems such a childish thing to do, but in a way our whole romance was childish. It was midsummer madness, I sometimes think, as if, like those moony characters in Shakespeare, we had been transformed into persons utterly unlike ourselves. We were—or had been—reasonably serious, mature people: diligent students, respectful, honest, law-abiding. Later, we spent much of the summer breaking into Yale buildings at night.

Why? I still don't know, really, except that it was breathtaking and thrilling. Summer lawlessness again. We were lovestruck—or I was, certainly—and a little out of our minds. Maybe, having been, both of us, awkwardly earnest and over-achieving adolescents— grinds, to use the slang from back then—we were enjoying a delayed rebellious phase. Or maybe we were under the spell of the weather. It was a hot, humid summer, as New Haven summers so often are, and the mugginess sometimes got to you and made you a little crazy.

The first place we broke into was the Payne Whitney gym. We went through a first-floor window that had been left partly open. It was as easy as that. It amazes me now to think that there was no security, no alarms. We were hyper, on edge, but not really worried about getting caught. We never even thought about it. If we had been apprehended, I realize now, the consequences could have been ruinous. Nancy might well have lost her teaching job. I could have lost my fellowship to study in England.

In those days, unlike now, the Yale campus was just about deserted in summer. The streets were empty; the great Gothic buildings were dark and silent. We wandered around as if visiting some abandoned medieval town cleared out by plague. The gym, one of the grandest buildings on campus, was built to look like a cathedral, and the tall clerestory windows let in just enough light for us to find our way around. We swam in the enormous pool and then jumped for a while on the trampoline, where we also made out for a bit, flopped there on the canvas. On another occasion, we somehow found our way to the rowing tanks—down in the basement—and practiced our rowing strokes. The only time we did any real damage was the evening we broke into Branford College—through a ground-floor window—and found ourselves in a dining-hall storeroom. Stacked on a shelf were some industrial-sized cans of sliced peaches, and we helped ourselves to one of them.

Looking back now, I barely recognize these two young people. Or, rather, I recognize them physically: he is skinny and bony, wearing blue jeans, an old blue button-down shirt, and penny loafers without socks; she is in a square-necked Norwegian fisherman's blouse, her long blond hair pulled back with a hippie-ish wood-and-leather barrette. What I can't understand is what on earth they were thinking.

A few weeks later, I asked Nancy to marry me. She said yes. I was twenty-one years old, she was twenty-two, and we had known each other for about six weeks. We had only the vaguest idea of what we wanted to do with our lives, and almost no notion at all of how we might support ourselves. Our last break-in that summer was into the Classics Department library, a room with a marble fireplace at the top of Phelps Gate. I trust that since then the Yale security people have tightened things up. We could have walked away with some very valuable books. The whole evening was a folly in a way. We stayed up practically all night, even though Nancy was to begin teaching the next morning. She showed up sleepless and ill prepared. Not an ideal start to adult life.

And yet fifty-odd years later, we are still married, still happy. Impulsive as we were, we must have sensed something about each other, some kind of unspoken compatibility. Our breaking and entering days were short-lived, and we have never done anything like that since. Our lives are almost comically unadventurous, although in the summer, we do loosen up a bit. Not that you would ever notice. Our routines then are almost as unvarying as those during the rest of the year. We come to the house and we do the same things: walk on the beach, go for a swim, take an afternoon sail, have a glass of wine on the deck. I'd like to think we're still the kind of people who are capable of breaking in somewhere, but who am I kidding?

Finding a Place

Nancy and I were about as unlike as the two Chips, and in many of the same ways. She was a WASP; I was Irish Catholic—even though I hadn't been to church in years. Her family was well-to-do, and mine was not. They lived in the Midwest; I was from New England. But, oddly, one of the things we had in common was a store of summer memories—mine from the Camp, hers from a couple of indelible summers spent with her family in Bristol, Rhode Island, and in nearby Little Compton. When our kids were young we used to join her parents for a week or two in that very pretty town, with its handsome stone walls and saltwater farms sloping down to the Sakonnet River. But after a couple of years of this we were determined to find a place of our own. I think at some level I was intent on re-creating the Camp. It never occurred to either one of us to take vacations the way so many other families did—to pile in the car and visit Disneyland, the Grand Canyon, the Jersey Shore. We wanted another home.

Nancy and I found our summer place on the south coast of Massachusetts, not far from what I think of as the Bermuda Triangle of the state, lots of woodsy little towns you've never heard of, where eighteenth-century farmhouses stand next door to Capes and raised ranches. The real secret of the place is its seeming ordinariness. It's beautiful but in an austere, understated way. There's a beach with sand dunes, but none as grand and dramatic as those in Wellfleet and Truro. There's a historic neighborhood where whaling captains used to live, but the houses are far more modest than those in Edgartown and Nantucket. There are some gentleman's farms, with carefully mown fields spooling down to the water like carpet, but just as many working farms, with tractors and hay-balers. You can drive by and smell manure. There are yachts in the harbor, but not the kind with bow thrusters and helicopter pads. Many spend the winter dry-docked in people's driveways. The biggest boats, by far, belong to the fishing fleet tied up at the town wharf—lobster boats and draggers. Tourists sometimes go down there to gawk, and the fishermen make an art of ignoring them. The wharf is a workplace, not a scenic attraction, except on Wednesday evenings, when people turn up from all over and play bluegrass music while sitting in camp chairs. There are no motels in town, no souvenir shops or motorbike rental places, and just a handful of restaurants, none of them memorable. For a fancy meal you've got to drive forty minutes at least. The people who live there year-round tolerate the summer folk but don't fawn over them. It used to be said that they threw a big party every September, after the summer invaders had packed up and gone home. "Skukes" is what they call us summer people—birds who foul the nests of others.

Not everyone gets this place. It may even be an acquired taste of sorts. Some people try it for a week or two and then never return. Others come back year after year, and so do their children and grandchildren. More than many summer towns, it's a family place. Singles would go out of their mind here. We found the place by accident—from a summer rental notice pinned to a bulletin board where I worked. There was no picture, just a description, and we took the place on faith. It proved to be a gray shingled cottage on a bank overlooking a wide expanse of water with a marsh

in the middle and woods way off on the other side—
a tidal estuary, though the locals called it a river. The
written description didn't do the place justice, but
even a photo, unless it was wide-angle, wouldn't have
added much. The impression you got, standing there,
was one of openness, expansiveness, and motion—the
water moving with the tide, the marsh grass bending
in the breeze, egrets fussily picking up their feet in
the shallows, like someone with good shoes trying to
navigate a puddle, and osprey hovering in the sky.

The house was no-frills—the only shower was
outdoors, by the basement door, and if you weren't
careful the shower curtain would blow open in the
breeze—but just fine for our purposes. We brought
some games and a huge box of wooden blocks and
the kids happily played for hours on a screened-in
sunporch that was the room we used most often.
Sarah was six that first summer and in the middle of
an intense *Little House on the Prairie* phase. She liked to
wear long sundresses and dabble in a nearby "spring"
she had discovered. Septic-tank overflow, actually, but
we were such summer-house rookies we didn't figure
that out for days. Ben was three and a half and, wor-
risomely, still in diapers. If he wasn't toilet-trained
by September, he wouldn't be allowed to enter the

nursery school Nancy had found for him, and that was unthinkable. She was counting on having a few free hours every morning starting that fall. So one of the high points of that summer was that I taught him to pee in a toilet. To get to that point we practiced outside a lot. That's another great thing about summer, if you're male and have property hidden from the road—you can relieve yourself outdoors as much as you like.

Newly independent, Ben took to wandering by himself down the lane to where a fisherman named Bud lived. They had long conversations—about fish, probably—and when I once apologized to Bud and said I hoped Ben wasn't a nuisance, he said, no, he enjoyed the company. It was around this time that Ben became obsessed with boats (the family affliction) and began making models of them—assemblages of bark and sticks that required globs and globs of gooey white Elmer's. You could tell a motorboat from a sailboat not so much by the absence of a mast as by a big glued-together mess at the back: an outboard.

These models were displayed on some concrete steps at the back of the house, which is also where the kids kept their shell collections. Those seemed to grow exponentially with every visit to the beach: there were a few delicate scallop shells, but mostly stacks and stacks of plate-sized surf clams bleached white by the sun. I used to collect them, too, on the few boyhood occasions when we went to the beach, but now wonder why. One clamshell looks pretty much like another, and on most beaches they're so plentiful that there's not much thrill in finding them. In my day at least, clamshells had a practical use. Grown-ups used them for ashtrays and were always grateful, or pretended to be, when you presented them with a nice new one. For some reason, though, children still insist on picking them up and bringing them home—souvenirs, I guess, or maybe the appeal is their very abundance.

We bought nets for the kids, and they spent hours at the water's edge, trying to scoop up crabs and minnows. The house came with a rowboat, a blue plywood pram, and at low tide we took it out to a sandbar where the kids could run around and jump in swimming holes—places where the sand dropped off, leaving deep little pools where the water reached over your head and was pleasingly cool. And we went to the beach, practically every day, and did all the things you do with children at the beach: wading, wave-jumping, sand-castle-building, burying them up to their necks in the sand. I don't think I was aware of it, but I can see now that I was beginning to make the transition from youthful, sometimes crazy summers to ones more sedate and grown-up, watching my kids learn how to do the very same things I used to do. I spent what now seems like hours watching bucket after bucket of water get dumped into a freshly dug hole and then seep away, and learned that it's possible to be bored half out of your mind and still have a pretty good time.

Jumping

The second summer after we met Chip he introduced us to bridge-jumping. The bridge in question is a thousand-foot-long span that crosses over the main channel leading to the harbor and connects the mainland to a barrier beach. It was built in 1958—replacing an earlier and lower drawbridge that was always holding up traffic—and I imagine people have been jumping off it ever since. Last June I saw about two dozen teenagers jump simultaneously, and I realized they must be high school kids marking the end of school, or maybe seniors celebrating graduation.

In general, Chip was less of a daredevil than I am—more concerned about propriety and appearances—and I don't think he had jumped for years himself. But the idea came up one night at dinner at our place when we were talking about crazy stuff people did. I told a story about scaring myself half to death once while rock-climbing in the Shawangunks—something I intend never to do again. Chip said, "Did you know that people sometimes jump off the bridge?"

Right away, I said, "Let's do it!" There had been wine with dinner, and I can't swear that wasn't a factor. But I also think it was an indication of how our friendship had progressed. We were comfortable enough with each other to begin to be a little reckless.

Chip went home and got his bathing suit. I changed into mine, loaded Nancy and the kids into the car, and drove to a little parking area just before the bridge—where Chip was waiting. For some reason, I made a point of shaking hands with each of the children, thus planting the notion that I might never come back. We walked up to the bridge. Chip pointed out a good spot, and, just like that, he was gone. Without hesitation he climbed over the railing and leaped out into the dark. I waited until I heard a splash and saw his head pop up below, and then I waited some more and some more after that.

The bridge is not all *that* high. The drop to the water varies a bit according to the tide but can't be more than thirty feet. But when you're standing there, looking down, thirty feet seems like a lot, especially at night. Nighttime is when a lot of people prefer to jump, because there's less boat traffic passing underneath and therefore less chance of your crashing through the roof of a slow-moving cabin cruiser. But in the dark the water below seems inky and fathomless, and standing there on the thin little strip of concrete on the other side of the guardrail, you feel as if you're looking into the abyss. By now everyone in the family—except the grandchildren—has made the leap at least once. The two Bens—our son and Chip's—have jumped close to two hundred times. There was one summer in their teens when that was practically all they did. I've also known several people to pause there for a long time, staring downward, and then think better of the whole enterprise and clamber back over the rail.

The secret, as with so many things in life, is not to think too much. You stand there for a moment, take a breath and hold it, and then, before you can change your mind, just let go and step out into the night. The surprise—every time—is how long it takes to drop. You find yourself thinking, Oh, this is much longer than I remembered, and wondering whether this was such a good idea after all. And then suddenly you hit the water with a slap and plunge downward.

Let's hope you aimed your jump properly and don't hit anything. I forgot to mention that the channel is fairly narrow and deepest, of course, at the middle. At low tide there's hardly any water near the edge. But the more toward the middle you jump, the longer your swim back, so it's tempting to want to cheat a little and pick a launching spot nearer the shore. I once misjudged and struck the bottom—where it was soft, thank goodness, and not with enough velocity to cause me more than a moment of terror.

A certain amount of terror is the whole point, of course. That long moment of free fall is both exhilarating and heart-thumpingly scary, and when your descent into the drink is finally arrested and you swim your way back up—claw your way is what it feels like—and break through the surface, inhaling a great, blessed breath of air, the feeling is one of indescribable relief. You're alive! You tread water for a moment, taking it all in—the lights on the shore, the waves lapping against the pilings, the occasional hum of a car passing on the bridge overhead—and feeling so happy and so relieved that you decide, Hey, let's do that again!

In daylight the whole experience seems more larksome, less otherworldly. You're jumping into water, reassuringly blue, glinting in the sun, not some dark and velvety ether. But the thrill is much the same, and so is the feeling of excitement when your head pops back up into the air. Your whole body tingles with alertness; the breaths you greedily take are so sweet you almost don't want to let them out again. You're alive—really, really alive; more alive than you know how to describe. Eventually this feeling passes, of course. If you remained that alive, aliveness would be intolerable. But it's pleasant to be reminded, every once in a while. What bridge-jumping amounts to is a way of ever so slightly risking your life—or maybe just pretending to risk your life—so that you can remind yourself again how grateful you are to have it.

This gratitude is all the sweeter the older one gets, though at a certain point it's also a little embarrassing to be caught out in search of it. I hadn't jumped from the bridge for ages when, a couple of years ago, I decided to see if I still could. I made it safely and was walking back to where I had parked when a police car pulled up. There are no signs specifically prohibiting bridge-jumping, but even so you try to do it when the police are not around. In this case, someone must have phoned them. The officer rolled down his window and said, "We heard people were jumping off the bridge. Have you seen anyone?"

"No," I replied. "I don't think so."

He looked me over. I had put my shirt and shoes back on, but my bathing suit was wet, and so was my hair. "So you're just going to stand there and lie to me?" the officer said. He shook his head. "At your age."

Snowdie

The summer we met Chip and Gay was the last summer we spent in the little gray shingled house. The landlord told us he wanted to use it for himself. This came as a blow, because in those days there wasn't much of a rental market in town. The Realtors—and there were many fewer back then—weren't interested in such short-term transactions, and there were no ads, nothing like VRBO or the Internet. We asked around, followed a few leads that led nowhere. It was Chip who saved us, by casually suggesting that we might want to rent Snowdie. That was the house on the hill across the water from us, where his family had spent their summers starting at the turn of the century. We went over there with Chip one afternoon, and fell in love as much with the history of the place as with the house itself—the idea that so many generations had spent their summers there. We rented it the following summer, and for twenty more summers after that.

By then Snowdie had drifted into a kind of genteel shabbiness, and was cluttered with castoffs. There was a Victorian sofa in the living room, so uncomfortable it must have been stuffed with horsehair, and a baby grand piano, badly out of tune, in the dining room. The bed Nancy and I slept in had a mattress also of horsehair, with a big trough in the middle. You would wake in the middle of the night thinking you had fallen into a trench. The kitchen was ramshackle and desperately underequipped, with exposed studs, open shelves, linoleum counters, and a sink with old-fashioned, T-shaped spigots. Over in a corner there lurked an old Hoovermatic washing machine, the kind with a mangle on top. If you weren't careful it would try to swallow your hand. And everywhere in the house there were chairs: rockers, bentwood chairs, Hitchcock chairs, Shaker chairs, armchairs, wing chairs, splat-back chairs, upholstered Victorian chairs with carving on top. Our kids once counted them all, and the total came to thirty-two.

Part of the pleasure of renting a summer place is the opportunity to peek into the life of another family. You look at the photographs on the end table, the portrait over the fireplace, the yellowing paperbacks left behind in the bedroom, the knickknacks in the corner cupboard (a little orchestra of ceramic frogs), the pewter tennis trophy on the sideboard, the old-fashioned shower cap hanging on a hook in the bathroom, and you think, Who *are* these people and what were their summers like? Do they resent our being here?

In the case of Snowdie, there were clues everywhere, especially in a volume of sermons I found, next to a complete set of the James Bond novels (a later addition, surely) and a history written by Chip's mother. The original inhabitants of the house, Chip's grandparents, were a family from Brooklyn, where the paterfamilias was a minister. They were summer pioneers of a sort, who discovered the area at the end of the nineteenth century and encouraged some clergy friends to build houses there too. I'm guessing they traveled on the night boat, a paddle-wheel steamer, that left New York every evening and arrived at dawn in Fall River. Dinner was served by uniformed stewards on real china and passengers slept in real staterooms. All this, not to mention the house itself, suggests a certain degree of wealth. Maybe ministers were paid better in those days? And what about the church in Brooklyn—did it just shut down for three months, allowing the parishioners to backslide into moral slackness?

Moral slackness never happened to Chip's forebears and their friends. They took summer seriously—made a religion of it, you could say. The wives, the matriarchs, became fierce botanizers. The ministers wrote books and sermons. They did the usual summer stuff—swam and sailed and went on picnics—but with a kind of fervor that compelled them to go outside and enjoy themselves even if the weather was bad. I liked to imagine them—the men in stiff collars and straw skimmers, their wives in long muslin dresses—strolling on the lawn and, like my mother, snuffling in big lungfuls of salt air and proclaiming it healthful and God-given. Unconsciously, I even picked up some of their summer seriousness. By the time we first rented Snowdie we had a boat, and I made a sort of moral imperative out of sailing. It was my job, I used to joke, and I went out almost every day, even if I didn't really feel like it. I always came back feeling virtuous.

Chip inherited from those forebears a need to be busy. Until he got sick, I never knew him to sleep late. It was as if he didn't want to miss a single day of his life. He once said of a mutual friend of ours, "That guy never sits still." The same, in a way, was true of him. He wasn't nervous and fidgety, like our friend—the opposite, in fact. He always seemed relaxed and unflustered, and he was perfectly capable of sitting down—for a while, anyway—and reading a book or watching TV. He wrote funny poems sometimes. He was also a good cartoonist and for a while tried submitting his drawings to *The New Yorker*. Most of them featured a character based on himself, square-faced, flat-nosed, tousle-haired, scratching his head over one screwup or another. In one, possibly revealing cartoon, I remember, this hapless guy was being commanded to "Stop rummaging around in your mind." Chip was yet to get sick, but a surprising number of his cartoons depicted surgical mishaps. There was even an entire strip consisting of step-by-step instructions for replacing your own hip.

But Chip was happiest when he was outdoors doing something. One summer he built an elaborate Japanese garden, complete with a pagoda-roofed teahouse. The summer after that he built a tree house with a door, windows, and a shingled roof. Sometimes, he'd take out his old Coast Guard sextant and shoot some sun sights—just to make sure the Earth hadn't moved. Much of our friendship consisted of simply doing things together. Chip was usually at his job when we were at Snowdie (his family took their vacation at the end of July and beginning of August, at a cabin

Chip's father had built on an island in Canada), but sometimes, when he was free, I'd show up at his place, which was close enough that I could walk or bike there. Or maybe he'd turn up at Snowdie. As often as not, we'd be dressed almost identically—khaki shorts and polo shirt of the same color. Telepathy maybe, or just proof of the smallness of our sartorial imaginations. On a Saturday morning if I arrived at his place with coffee and the paper, we might sit there for a while and look at the headlines. He might flick on ESPN for a quick check of the scores. And then we'd make a plan: Sailing? Golf? Gathering a bunch of quahogs? Sometimes we just did chores. Sanding boats, hauling them around on trailers. Finding a lost mooring by wading around in the mud at low tide. A quick swim maybe, or a trip to the driving range. It reminded me of boyhood summers, when the great question every morning was "What do you want to do today?" and you had to think of something, even if it was just the same thing you thought of the day before.

You could argue, I suppose, that all this running around and obsessively pursuing summer activities was really a kind of displacement, a way of keeping our minds off more important things. We didn't talk much, and when we did, we almost never shared anything of real importance. We sometimes did Three

Stooges imitations, and Chip, if he chose, could talk for extended stretches exactly like Donald Duck, a knack I never came close to mastering. A lot of our time together was spent in companionable silence, or else in conversations that could have been scripted by Larry David:

"If you were on death row, what would you want as your last meal?"

"I don't know. Swordfish maybe? Corn on the cob?"

"Yeah, but think about the kind of swordfish they'd have in prison. You might be better off with McDonald's."

"A nice steak?"

"They'd overcook it. Maybe just a hot dog—they couldn't screw that up."

"Maybe you should just pass? You're probably not going to feel like eating anyway."

I once interviewed Jane Fonda, and somehow we got off onto the differences between male and female friendship. "Here's the whole problem with men," she said. "They don't talk." She may be right. Almost everything I know I know from books, and in all the ones I've read there's not a lot about male friendship. The great exception is Huck and Jim, of course, but that's not a friendship between equals. Most male friendship—literary male friendship, that is—seems to take place during wartime, and it consists largely of badinage. Think of *A Farewell to Arms* or, even better, the crazy, bantering comradeliness of *Catch-22*. Or else there's just silence. I've been rereading the *Aeneid* recently and have been struck by the character of Achates—or *fidus Achates,* as he's always called, faithful or trusty Achates, Aeneas's right-hand man. That's practically all we know about him: that he's dog-loyal. In the whole poem I don't think he speaks more than half a dozen lines. That's partly because Aeneas is meant to be the star here, and the poem is at pains to emphasize the solitary nature of his quest. But I think Virgil is also on to something else: the comfort and reassurance of being in the company of someone who doesn't require anything more of you than your presence.

Some things about Chip I learned over time: Unlike me, he wasn't particularly driven, or concerned about his place in the world. He was a talented, conscientious architect, but he hated the part of the job that required him to drum up business. He wasn't a very interior person, or not that you could discern. He liked to make fun of introspection and was very good at changing the subject when something that he didn't want to talk about came up. I can honestly say that I never once saw him angry, or even in a lousy mood.

He must have had his bad moments, but he kept them to himself.

I'm pretty much the opposite, a little obsessive, a brooder and a pessimist, and so I loved his open, uncomplicated nature, his enthusiasm. I happily bought into his upbeat vision of things. And I wasn't the only one who felt this way. I eventually discovered that he had a whole circle of fans and devotees, people attracted, as I was, by his warmth, curiosity, and kindness. He was so modest and self-effacing that I don't think he ever grasped how many people looked up to him.

Chip was also capable of silliness—like his Snowdie forebears, it turned out. Nancy and I once came upon a chest there filled with a strange collection of mothball-smelling clothing: bits of military uniforms, a policeman's cap and tunic, a fisherman's slicker and sou'wester, housecoats, bathrobes, crinolines, straw hats, a bowler, a pith helmet, a couple of fedoras, one of those old mink stoles with the mink's head still attached, a pair of suspendered trousers so tremendous that a child could fit in each leg. There were also walking sticks, a lantern, a cricket bat, broken tennis rackets, and a lot of other random stuff.

"What on earth is all this junk?" I asked Chip.

"Oh, that," he said. "It's for charades."

"Charades?"

He explained that his grandparents and their friends had played a form of charades in which teams of people would dress up in costumes and act out the syllables of a word in little skits. There had been an annual charades party at Snowdie, to which people would contribute old clothes and props. Chip came up with the idea of resurrecting the custom, and so for the next several years our two families had a charades party. We mailed out written invitations—in some instances to people old enough to remember the original parties. Nancy and Gay and the kids baked chocolate-chip cookies and made lemonade, because those were the original refreshments. Chip and I visited junk shops and Goodwill stores in search of supplementary props and outfits.

We observed the lemonade-only rule the first year, but then deviated from orthodoxy and added beer and wine (to the displeasure of some of the old-timers). The other rule we broke was the one about children, who were excluded from the original charades parties, possibly on the grounds that it would be too shocking for them to see their elders dressed up in costumes and acting foolish. I wish I could remember more of the words acted out on those hilarious evenings, but the only one that sticks in mind—probably because it's a little unusual—is *contumely*. The rules required that the word be acted out syllable by syllable, with a final skit dramatizing the whole word. So in this case the first act—*con*—was a gang of costumed convicts roped together. Act II—*tume*—was an entombment, a mock burial, with a child, clad all in black, carried out on the shoulders of some grown-ups and then laid to rest on the floor while crazily dressed mourners heaped dirt on him with imaginary shovels. Act III—*ly*—was a sailing scene. A crew came out, dressed in naval motley, and took their places in an imaginary sailboat; when the captain, wearing an old-fashioned admiral's hat, spun his pretend wheel, his crew ducked to avoid an invisible boom swinging over and leaned sharply to one side. Get it? No one there did, even people familiar with the sailing command that usually announces the beginning of a tack: "Ready about. Hard a-lee." The last act was easier: everyone pointing at each other and gibbering soundlessly.

In retrospect, *contumely* was much too hard a word, and I fear it may have been my suggestion. The skits, on the other hand, were all Chip's idea, and everyone enjoyed them, the children especially. Far from being shocked, they were thrilled to be included in another kind of summer misrule. While Snowdie for me had overtones of earnestness and self-improvement, for our kids it was a place of freedom and liberation. Scattered around the hill were other, smaller buildings maintained by other members of the family. One was called the Duckery, and I think that early on it may really have been one—a place for breeding ducks. Another was a shed, but it housed a family of four. I'm not sure it even had plumbing. But these other houses all came with kids, and ours quickly became part of a pack that also included Chip's children and eventually—as everyone got older—some teenage boys who lived nearby and a girl who worked as a summer au pair for a family down the lane.

They had the kind of summers I remembered from the Camp: out the door first thing in the morning, back for lunch (or maybe not), home for supper, and then sometimes out yet again for flashlight tag or hide-and-seek—all with little or no adult supervision. When the kids were old enough we even let them take the boat out alone, or tool around—without life jackets—in a little outboard we acquired. If they wanted to go to the beach, we dropped them off. We didn't know about helicopter parenting then, and I'm just as glad.

In my head there is a home movie of those years in which all the kids on that hill grow up before my eyes. Sarah and her friends get tanner, tawnier, prettier, and more coltish, and pretty soon they're teenagers, with crushes and whispered secrets. The two Bens play endless games of Wiffle Ball, and as they get older and taller and lose that little-boy elfinness, the boundaries have to be changed because the hits go so much farther. More and more balls are lost in a towering pine tree down the left-field line. They may be up there still.

It was during those Snowdie years that I learned the second lesson of adult summering: that at a certain point, much as you love watching your children, you also have to let them not be watched. Their summers are their own. And there's a sad corollary, one I won't dwell on: your gradual realization that they will never love you as much as you love them.

Snowdie summers meant as much to our kids as they did to Nancy and me. To this day, they're still close to the friends they made back then, even though their grown-up lives have all taken very different directions. When they get together, as they tend to do every summer, they just pick up where they left off, all those years ago. They also imagine Snowdie-like summers for their own kids, our grandchildren, though I fear those kinds of summers may be drawing to a close. Who has the time today? Nancy, though she ran her own business, was essentially a stay-at-home mom. And I had a job, unusual then, that enabled me to do some of my work from Snowdie, so our vacations were a little longer and more leisurely than most. Now, except for the two weeks or so that our grandkids spend with us, they have the modern kind of summer, every minute programmed and accounted for: lessons, camps, playdates, traveling teams. And even their visits with us have a kind of urgency—a need to cram everything in and a dread of idle moments. The children whirl through the house, leaving their stuff everywhere: their Legos, their ninjas, their flip-flops, their swim masks and flippers. They're always hungry but never finish eating anything. There are half-eaten sandwiches and half-drunk cans of seltzer, now warm and flat, everywhere you look. Don't misunderstand me. We love it when they come. We also love the restoration of order when they go.

Blowing Stuff Up

The Fourth of July is one of my favorite days of the year. I love everything about the Fourth—the flags, the bunting, the parade in our little town: an endless line of fire trucks blaring their sirens, and local dignitaries riding in open cars, hurling candy at children watching shyly from the edge of the road. There are no bands, as Nancy often laments, but on the other hand, lots and lots of tractors.

But what I really love are the fireworks. My family thinks that this passion of mine is a little twisted, because the summer I turned thirteen, I was badly burned—not from fireworks, but from an exploding blowtorch—and spent three months in the hospital. I lost a whole summer of my life, in effect, and perhaps that accounts for why summers are so important to me now. I was sometimes in great pain, sometimes just bored and lonely. I still have extensive scars from back then, though I'm less self-conscious about them than I used to be. (One of the very few benefits of getting older, at least for me, is that in the general wax-melt that starts in middle age—the facial sagging, the loosening of the packing around the jowls, the drooping of the eyelids, the pooling up of excess flesh under the chin—we all start looking like accident victims.)

You'd think I would now be wary of fire in any form, but if anything, my accident has made me a little reckless. I love blowing stuff up. Computerized, industrial-strength fireworks—like the show Macy's puts on every year in New York City, with shells blasting in sync with symphonic music—are what many people think of when they think of the Fourth. Or maybe they think of local fireworks in the town or county park: blankets on the grass, little kids crying, dogs sniffing in the picnic basket, a Grucci- or Zambelli-orchestrated show that ends with a finale that sounds like an air raid. Whomp, whomp, whomp—until you want to shout with pleasure.

I never experienced a show like that until I was an adult. Most fireworks, in my day, were modest and do-it-yourself. Growing up, Tom and I had sparklers, which could be made to trace lacy patterns in the dark, and eventually firecrackers, which were far too precious to be shot off in bunches. From an older kid, we would buy single packs, wrapped in red tissue paper, for the outrageously jacked-up, black market price of a dollar, and then carefully unbraid them, so that the crackers could be shot off individually. To light up a whole pack at once, the way firecrackers are meant to be used, in a crackling, ear-popping salvo, the entire bunch of them hopping on the pavement, was unthinkable. Ignited one by one, savored, a pack's worth of crackers could occupy an entire afternoon. There was the thrilling moment of ignition, when the fuse finally glowed red, sizzling and sputtering sparks, and then that exquisite moment of suspense before the ka-boom. You could hold a lit firecracker, your heart pounding, in your hand for as long as you dared before tossing it. You could also fret over the inevitable duds, waiting and waiting to see if the fuse might just be slow, which sometimes it was, the firecracker blowing up practically in your face as you anxiously bent over it. The danger, together with the illegality, was part of the thrill, as was the sulfury gunpowder smell— the smell of hellfire and brimstone, I liked to imagine, which suggested hell might not be as bad as they said.

For a while as an adult I was fascinated with novelty fireworks—earthbound ones, usually, that scooted along the ground or hovered just above it, imitating butterflies or hopping frogs or buzzing bees, or, in one amazing instance, that seemed to reenact the entire story of civilization. This particular firework was given to me by a friend, and I have never seen anything like it again. It was Chinese and came wrapped in an artful little tissue paper package that gave no clue to what was inside. I lit the fuse and for a while it just fizzled. Then everything happened at once: bangs, pops, whistles, showers of sparks. A pause, and from the smoldering wreckage a little yellow house or pagoda silently arose, story by story, until it stood about six inches high. Each story was illuminated by miniature cellophane windows, which glowed from within for several seconds, and then the lights dimmed and flickered and went out, leaving the house pooled in darkness there on the lawn—a tiny monument to something or other.

But what I most relish now is height and noise—rockets that soar up into the summer night and then explode like a cannon shot into an umbrella of sparks that slowly drift earthward. I'm talking about near-professional-quality fireworks, and I learned from Chip that you can actually buy this stuff legally. Naively, I had assumed that fireworks could be purchased only on the down-low, and in a way, that, too, was part of the thrill. In the years before meeting Chip I used to go down to Chinatown, where fireworks were not sold openly, exactly, but were not hard to find. If you stood around looking aimless for long enough, someone would come up to you—the way people did uptown, whispering about the availability of "loose joints"—and ask if you were interested in fireworks. This, I should add, was before Mayor Rudy Giuliani cracked down on fireworks and the market for them vanished almost overnight. Typically, you'd be led to the back of a Chinese grocery, where for fifty bucks or so you could fill a shopping bag with firecrackers, bottle rockets, Roman candles—all the essentials. One year, though, my guide, my fireworks Virgil, was not a Chinese guy but a burly Italian man who led me out of Chinatown and into a part of Little Italy where I had never been. The streets were dark and quiet, seemingly blocks away from the brightly lit, touristy part of Little Italy, where all the restaurants are, and the more we walked, the more anxious I grew. We came to a tenement, and, thinking it was a dumb thing to do but not wanting to offend the guy, I followed him up several flights. As he climbed the stairs in front of me, his untucked shirt rode up a bit and I could see a gun stuffed in the waistband of his pants. I was certain now that I was going to be robbed, maybe even shot. We stopped outside a door where there was a handwritten sign, in an almost childish scrawl, that said "Dentists

Office," and he indicated I should go in. Expecting to feel a pistol butt cracking against the back of my skull, I did, and found myself in what amounted to Aladdin's cave. There were fireworks everywhere, stacks of them and in more variety than I had ever imagined. Two very cheerful women took my fifty bucks and helped me with my selections, and then Virgil led me downstairs and indicated the way back to Chinatown. On the way home to New Jersey, my heart kept going off in little flare-bursts of happiness and relief—and pride. Not only had I scored some fireworks, but I'd scored them from a guy packing heat!

On the Fourth itself, however, I disgraced myself. Among the many offerings in that magical dental suite were M80s, much thicker and more powerful than an ordinary firecracker. They look like miniature sticks of dynamite, which for all practical purposes they are. I'd bought a few, naturally, and on the afternoon of the Fourth, bored and impatient for evening to come, so that I could get down to some serious igniting, I decided to see what would happen if I tossed a lit M80 into our mailbox and then shut the little metal door. It went off with a whomp like a mortar and blew the mailbox off its post. Not long after, I heard sirens and turned tail, running down the driveway and hiding in the garage, while poor Nancy, who had been gardening out in front of the house, had to greet the police and take the rap. That evening she got tired of watching me light off Roman candles and, satisfied that I wasn't going to blow up the house, turned off the kitchen light and went to bed. I still had a handful of bottle rockets left and set them off one by one. The last one rose up over the roof, soared above the hemlocks in the backyard, and bathed the driveway in an unearthly red. I remember feeling happy but also a little stupid—a middle-aged guy lighting off fireworks all by himself—and thinking that only Chip would understand.

Because Chip grew up in New Hampshire, where fireworks are legal, he had a much simpler history with them. If you wanted fireworks you went to the store and bought some. It was at his suggestion that we began driving every year to the Phantom Fireworks outlet in Seabrook, New Hampshire, the first town over the state line. We would also stop at the state liquor store nearby, where we would buy some whiskey and a couple of cigars to complete the alcohol, tobacco, and firearms trifecta. In time, especially after Chip got sick, those drives became a part of the Fourth of July ritual, almost as important as the fireworks themselves.

The Phantom store—the very same one, as it hap-

pens, where the Tsarnaev brothers, the Boston Marathon bombers, stocked up—was a revelation. It wasn't
like those convenience stores you sometimes find in
Rhode Island or Connecticut, where low-grade fireworks are legal and where sparklers and bottle rockets are sold, pretty tame stuff, along with cigarettes,
chewing tobacco, lottery tickets, and twenty-seven
kinds of beef jerky. It was a genuine fireworks supermarket. You went in, showed them a driver's license,
picked up a shopping cart, just as you would at the
A&P, and wandered the long aisles, where stacked on
the shelves was a range of goods even more remarkable than those at that Little Italy cave: sparklers,
poppers, rockets, salutes, crackers by the brick and
half-brick, Roman candles, ground spinners, aerial
spinners, smoke bombs, pinwheels, parachutes, flam-
ing spears, fiery frogs, reloadable mortars, and row
after row of cardboard boxes, the size of wine cartons,
containing ten, twenty, thirty shells or more. The variety was so great it was dizzying. How do you choose?
We used to rely a lot on the graphics and the names on
the boxes. Bada Bing, Bada Boom—how can you say
no? The Motherload, that sounded pretty good, and
so did the Tunguska Blast and Tropic Thunder. The
store used to have a perpetual two-for-the-price-of-
one sale, so you wound up with twice as much as you

intended. We used to fill the back of Chip's van, but that's nothing compared with what I saw the last time I was at Phantom, when four or five employees were wheeling out carts full of merchandise—not just the big-box stuff, but a little of everything, even the fiery frogs—and, under the direction of a big bearded guy wearing cammies, helping load it into a repurposed yellow school bus with all the seats removed. I took one of the Phantom people aside and asked how much all this stuff had cost. "I'm not sure," he said. "I think about five thousand bucks." So naturally I had to go up and ask the bearded guy, "What are you going to do with all this?" He looked at me and said, without smiling, "I could tell you. But then I'd have to kill you."

Chip and I would drive our cargo home—or, strictly speaking, smuggle it, since carrying fireworks across the Massachusetts state line is illegal—congratulating ourselves for being so foresighted and well prepared. And then, usually after a cookout on the Fourth, we would light the stuff off with great solemnity. One year we did it down at the dock at the foot of the Snowdie hill. Not a great idea. A lot of the neighbors, including some of his relatives, freaked out, imagining they were under attack. Most of the time we used a field, across the street from Chip's house, that was owned by an accommodating neighbor. Early the next morning we would have to go over there and painstakingly pick up all the detritus—tiny scraps of paper, some of them almost confetti-size, and dozens and dozens of little white cardboard discs. Cleaning up could take more than an hour and leave you with a sore back, but it seemed a small price to pay.

Messing About in Boats

I now light off the fireworks at our dock, which we share with several other families. From there on a weekend summer afternoon you can watch an amazing array of watercraft go by. Little runabouts, Boston Whalers, inflatable Zodiacs, small cabin cruisers, some serious sport-fishing boats, with radar and flybridges and extra-long trolling rods. A few sailboats. Lots and lots of bright-colored kayaks. There seem to be more and more of them every year, singles and doubles, sometimes just gliding along with the current, sometimes furiously paddled by the kind of Patagonia-clad people who look like they've just come from a fifty-mile sprint on their racing bikes. You also see the odd rowing shell, perilously narrow, swept along so gracefully by those long, rhythmic oar strokes that you feel it might take flight at any moment. Like kayaks, the shells are a relatively new phenomenon. You didn't use to see them at all. In the annoying watercraft category are the Jet Skis, noisy and driven by reckless idiots (though secretly I suspect that riding one is probably a lot of fun), and more and more party boats—those squarish pontoon vessels that are basically floating patios. If I had access to torpedoes, I'd gladly sink them.

From all this waterborne traffic, which gets busier every season, you could conclude that for many people boating is right up there with swimming as a summer essential. It's an even newer phenomenon. For centuries people ventured out on the water only when they had to: to fish, to travel, to make war on each other. Shelley and Byron—Romantics in more ways than one—both liked to sail just for fun, but they were in the minority and also wealthy. Boating—or, rather, yachting, we should say—was a pastime pursued mostly by the well-to-do. It didn't really catch on as a popular form of recreation until after the Second World War, when advances in mass production and, especially, the development of fiberglass made boats more affordable.

My father, from whom I must have inherited my love of boats, hated fiberglass with a passion. I'm not sure why, exactly, because he certainly approved of affordability. I'm also not sure where his boat craziness came from. His family were not boaters. The dread Mac had no hobbies at all as far as I could tell. But for some reason my father was fascinated by boats. He was mildly obsessed, for example, with the story of Noah and the Ark and brought it up often, pointing out that though God had promised never again to destroy the world by flood, that didn't rule out nuclear war. My father was not a literalist, exactly, but a man of very practical imagination, and many of the details in the story bothered him. How could Noah build such an ark with just his three sons? Without power tools it would have taken them decades, and just what was "gopher wood" anyway? How did they herd all those animals, and once the creatures were all on board, what prevented them from eating each other? What did Noah and the crew do about the prodigious amounts of shit that would have piled up? But even so I think the notion of forty days afloat had great appeal to my father—to be secure and self-sufficient in a brand-new vessel of your own making, followed by a complete reboot in which you could start your life all over again. It was my father's version of a sea change.

During the war my father served on a minesweeper in the Navy, and that may be where he caught the bug, or it may be that he enlisted in the Navy in the first place because he wanted to go to sea. I don't know whether he elected to serve on a minesweeper, but it's possible, even though a minesweeper would not be most people's first choice. They were not infrequently blown up by the very mines they were sweeping for. But minesweepers were made of wood, so they'd be less apt to set off a magnetic trigger, and wooden boats were the only kind my father had any use for.

There used to be a little wicker box in our dining room sideboard. I think it was probably meant to be a sewing box, but my parents used it to store wartime memorabilia—letters and photographs. When I was young I liked to take it out and study the contents. There were several photos of my father in his Navy uniform—skinny, a little gawky—and one taken in Hawaii, where he was based for a while, of him and two other guys in Hawaiian shirts. They're grinning and look a little pie-eyed, and that picture connects with something I learned later: that my father and some of his buddies used to make bootleg hooch. He was scared to death, mostly—that came through in the letters he sent to my mother, to whom he was engaged by then. He talked about how lonely he was, and asked her to be more affectionate in her letters back to him. No such luck. Her letters to him weren't distant, exactly, but were perfunctory in their endearments. Mostly she talked about how much fun she was having—about outings to the beach with the girls at work, and ski trips to North Conway, New Hampshire, when on the train someone would break out a "jug," someone else a ukulele, and there would be a tipsy sing-along. I doubt her intent was cruel. She sometimes behaved this way to us when we were kids if we seemed too needy, reminding us that life goes on and self-pity is pointless. But sitting there on the dining room floor, my back against the sideboard, I used to picture my father, braced in his bunk, with the ship rolling in Pacific swells, reading and rereading those letters, looking for some sign that if he just got through this war the rest of his life would be better.

Practically the first thing he did, after he and my mother married, and while she was still pregnant with me, was build a boat, a plywood pram, in the living room of their rented apartment. And then he was unable to get it out the front door. I learned this from my mother, who was opposed to the project from the beginning and often brought it up as an example of my father's impractical dreaminess. During this same period, he also built a custom toy box for his unborn first child—me—and a little car, with working steering, later known as the Teeny Weenie. It seems to me now that he may have been in a slightly manic building phase to offset his anxiety about impending father-hood, or maybe he knew he would never have so much time on his hands again. How the boat was eventually extricated from the living room my mother never said, but it became our Camp boat, powered by one of those tiny, old-fashioned outboards with no cowling to conceal the engine parts. It always reminded me of an eggbeater. And then one summer the boat was no longer there. The plywood began to delaminate and it grew too leaky. I've owned two plywood prams to which this has happened. One I burned in a sort of Viking funeral; the other was beached on the lawn for a couple of years and served as a sandbox for the grandchildren until it became soggy and weed-infested. I chainsawed it into pieces and consigned it, too, to the flames. Our dinghy now, I'm ashamed to say, is made of fiberglass.

All that remained of my father's boat was the out-board, which lived for years in our basement and miraculously continued to run. Every now and then he'd bolt it to a trash can filled with water and tug on the pull rope until it fired up. My father often talked about getting another boat but never did until near the end of his life. When I was little he window-shopped instead, taking my brother and me down to the bank of the Charles River in Watertown, eyeing the handsome cabin cruisers that were moored there. We'd compare their merits, while idly tossing stones in the water, and then decide at length which one we'd like to own and whether we'd want to repaint it or not.

My father also read a lot of boating magazines, a habit I picked up, and even sent away for plans. He was a very good amateur woodworker. For years, he nurtured the dream of building another, bigger boat. His original notion was to build with wood, of course, but when I was in my teens, he suddenly and inexplicably embraced aluminum— beer cans, to be exact. Or maybe it wasn't so inexplicable. My father spent a lot of time in the basement. It was his refuge from my mother. He put on an old Navy fatigue jacket he kept there and puttered around, working on what he called his inventions, most of which never came to much. The best of them was the Wankel rotary engine, which he genuinely believed he thought of before Felix Wankel did, though Wankel in fact patented his design in 1929 and had built a working prototype by the late fifties, just about when my father was getting started. He never advanced much beyond making a lot of drawings—he was a skilled mechanical draftsman, with beautiful, meticulous handwriting—and casting a few metal parts in a mold he built.

While he worked down there in the basement, my

father liked to smoke (though he eventually gave that up) and drink beer. I never once saw him show the effects, but in the course of a long afternoon, he could put away the better part of a six-pack, and over time the empties piled up. He kept them in what had once been a coal bin before the house was converted to oil heat. I think in the beginning he was embarrassed there were so many, but then he began saving beer cans with a purpose. His plan was to use them as flotation for a pontoon boat. It pains me to think so now, but what he must have had in mind was a prototype of the floating patio!

This was the period when, sadly, we were growing apart, and soon I was off to college and seldom visited the basement anymore. But I think the idea was to somehow meld or solder the cans together into long tubes that could then be inserted into pontoons to make them more buoyant. He invented a gizmo, I know, to remove the tops of the cans—he began back before there were pull-tops, and you opened a beer with two triangular punches made with a church key—but maybe the bottoms were left intact. I wish now I had paid more attention. But for whatever reason—except, surely, a shortage of cans—the project never came to fruition. My father's next invention was a gadget that didn't just crumple beer cans but crushed them flat, so that they were like little metallic wafers.

He was by then a pretty unhappy man, hard of hearing (especially when my mother was talking), pinched for money, bored by his job, and lugging around a beach ball–sized paunch on his once slender frame. But a couple of years before his heart attack he came into a small windfall—a modest inheritance from a couple of maiden cousins the rest of us never even knew about. I'm sure my mother had her own ideas about what to do with the money, but somehow my father prevailed, and he bought himself a boat, a little Chris-Craft runabout made of mahogany plywood. It was so brightly varnished that, out of the water, it looked like a piece of furniture, and my father treated it that way. He used to trailer it to the Charles River and cruise that very stretch where we had admired the cabin cruisers years before, and then, back in the driveway, he would hose it down and rub the hull dry with a chamois. Never has a boat been more loved. I sometimes thought he regretted having to get it wet in the first place.

The Scituate house, where my parents moved in 1978, had a big, airy basement, but my father never set up shop there. The urge to make things had abandoned him. And Scituate Harbor, and the bay outside, was no place for his little Chris-Craft, designed for lakes and rivers. I went out with him once, trying to navigate from Scituate to nearby Humarock, and it got pretty hairy, with waves coming in over the stern. Somehow the saltwater also proved less congenial to the boat's engine, an ancient 25-horse Mercury that had always been the Achilles' heel of this venture. Even the boat's previous owner told my father it needed to be replaced. In Scituate it became balkier than ever, and the boat no longer went out much but just sat there in the driveway on its trailer. It was there the morning he died.

My first boat was a wooden sailboat. The wooden part would have pleased my father, and I like to imagine that he would thoroughly approve of my own boating obsession, which is now even greater than his. Every now and then, though I am now fifteen years older than he was when he died, I still see my father on the street, or someone who for an instant looks just like him, the same tilt of the head, the same way of tugging at his right ear, and I fantasize about grabbing his arm, Ancient Mariner fashion, and bringing him up to date. With so much in common these days, we would get along, I like to imagine, the way we did when I was a child. Among other things, we now have fatherhood in common. In my most extreme daydreaming, my father and I even go for a sail together, though the sailing part would be a novelty. For all his love of boats, I don't think he was ever on one that sailed. There was only one sailboat on the lake at the Camp, a wooden tub that the teenage boy who lived across the street from us found somewhere and fixed up. It was tied up next to the dock where we went swimming, and it only went out once that I recall. It drifted for a while and then had to be paddled back. I don't think the boy who owned it had any idea how to sail, and even if he had, the lake, long and narrow, with steep, wind-bending hills, wouldn't have been very congenial. Whatever happened to that sailboat? It leaked pretty badly, and could have sunk, for all I know.

The sailing bug came to me independently, and I'm still not sure quite how. As a young teenager I learned to sail, in a sort of half-assed fashion, at the Community Boat House on the Charles River, which offered instruction to Boston schoolkids for something like a dollar a year. The boathouse had a fleet of Mercurys, which you were allowed to take out on your own, first with just a mainsail and then, as you moved up the instruction ladder, with a jib and even a spinnaker. I was never spinnaker-rated. I was barely jib-qualified, and the high point of my Charles River career was somehow getting stuck against the low-arching Longfellow Bridge on an outgoing tide. The boat tried to drift underneath but was held up by the mast, jammed against the stonework. A launch had to come get me, and by the time I was pulled off, there was a sideways bend in the mast. It looked like a Brancusi sculpture. My humiliation was such that I never went back.

But by the time I was in my thirties I had developed a desire for a sailboat of my own, despite my childhood humiliation. So in our second summer in the gray shingled house I bought a used Beetle. Beetles are small catboats—boats with a single sail, that is, attached to a mast that is way up in the bow of the boat. In that respect they resemble a child's drawing of a sailboat, except that a child would never think to include the gaff—a spar, attached to the top of the sail, that gets hoisted up until it's almost parallel to the mast and sticking above it. The resulting sail shape is less the familiar triangle than a sort of trapezoid. All sailboats looked this way until the early twentieth century, when technology began to allow for masts that were much taller and stronger and didn't need a gaff to extend their height.

The drawback to the catboat rig is that the big single sail can be a lot to handle in a breeze, and with the sail so far forward, the bow always wants to turn toward the wind. You have to work sometimes—really lean on the tiller handle—to keep on course. The advantage of the rig is that, with the mast way up in the bow, you can have a big, beamy cockpit with plenty of room for passengers or cargo, or for lobster traps or fishing nets. For most of the nineteenth century, before the advent of the internal combustion engine, catboats were the workboats of New England. They also had centerboards, not deep keels, which suited them to the shoal waters in these parts.

The Beetle's very shallow draft makes it an ideal vessel for our river, which is in places only a few inches deep at low tide, but in other ways it's not so practical. A Beetle nowadays is pretty expensive for its size. For the same money you can buy a much bigger fiberglass boat, which might be easier to sail and will require much less upkeep. A lot of us continue to love these boats is precisely because they're old-fashioned, and because they're a link to an older, more traditional way of boatbuilding. The boat gets its name from the Beetle Company, a nineteenth-century New Bedford firm that specialized in building whaleboats—those long, narrow dories that whaling ships used to lower into the water after spotting a whale.

Whaleboats were relatively light, so they could be rowed quickly and hoisted easily, and they took a lot of bashing. Whaleships stopping in New Bedford, then the capital of the whaling industry, often needed whaleboat replacements, and the great claim of the Beetle Company was that they could build you one in just forty-eight hours. They could do this because they had figured out an early form of mass production. All Beetle whaleboats were the same, built upside down over the same mold, and many of the pieces—the hull planks, the spars, the rudder—were precut and shelved, awaiting assembly. When the whaling industry finally petered out, the Beetle Company embraced the trend of recreational boating, then still in its infancy, and came up with a design for a small, inexpensive knockoff of the classic Cape Cod catboat—the Beetle. The design has changed virtually not at all in more than a hundred years, and the boats are still built the same way, using the original patterns and molds and many parts that have been cut or fashioned in advance. They're the last mass-produced wooden boats still being sold—if you can call a dozen or so a year mass production.

Beetles look like little ships. They're short—about thirteen feet—and beamy, and very solidly built. The frames are steam-bent white oak, and the beautiful high coaming, one of the boat's most distinctive features, is also oak. The planks are cedar and even after decades retain their sweet, distinctive scent. If you close your eyes while sitting in the cockpit, you can imagine that you're sitting in a pencil sharpener. You sit on the floor, by the way—there are no benches—or else, if it's blowing, with your butt up on the coaming, where you can see the lovely way the hull sweeps around from the stern and up a little by the bow. *Sheer* is what boatbuilders call such a curve, and together with the boat's full, round bottom, it makes a Beetle seem almost delicate—a little like a slipper shell. While sailing, the boat is more powerful than graceful. It's too heavy to plane and so just pushes water out of the way, with a bow wave that's the marine equivalent of a snowplow's spray. But out on the mooring it floats lightly, easily, bobbing on the waves like a duck.

I bought my Beetle from a guy known as the Commander, because that was the rank he once held in the Coast Guard. He was a tall, somewhat imperious man, who wore a sort of khaki uniform all the time and kept a big trawler in the harbor, which he drove around as if standing on the bridge of a cutter. The Beetle he kept moored off his house, which was not far from where ours is now, and where he made a big operation of raising the American flag every day. I know I inspected the boat before handing over my check, but in my eagerness I apparently didn't notice that it leaked. Or maybe the Commander timed my arrival with a thorough pumping and sponging out of the Beetle. In any event the leaking got worse over the three or four years we owned it. By the end, I had to pump it out every day or so, and when Nancy and I sailed it, we sometimes wore foul-weather pants, in anticipation of the moment when water would start seeping up through the floorboards. But I loved that boat possibly more even than I loved its replacement, a brand-new Beetle, which when we took delivery of it seemed almost dazzling in its perfection. For a couple of seasons I was almost too nervous to sail it, fearful that I would hit a rock or have some mishap that would ding the hull or sully the immaculate finish. But that first Beetle seemed comfortable and homey, even though for some reason I painted the deck canvas a ridiculous maroon color. I still remember the day I picked it up—the first time I had ever sailed a Beetle on my own—and navigated it all the way down the river, past the two big rocks, and under the bridge. After all these years the bridge part of that journey is still a little terrifying to me. What if you run out of wind while you're underneath? What if the mast and upraised gaff won't fit under the span? As you look up from the cockpit, foreshortening makes it seem as if there's only an inch or two to spare, and sometimes that's true, as I discovered just this summer, when I tried going through not one of the tallest slots, but a slightly lower one, and slammed the gaff into the bridge—not unlike, come to think of it, my disaster on the Charles all those years ago. But somehow I got my new (old) boat up to its mooring—a giant block of cement Chip had helped me pour, inscribed, while the cement was still wet, with the initials of our whole family. Every couple of hours I would just go out and look at it, wondering at my good fortune. This was the boat my children learned to sail in, and the one our whole family explored the river in, sometimes eating lunch or supper picnics while gliding along. In my mind's eye this is often how I picture our then young family, with the kids bravely taking turns to climb up on the deck and stand in front of the mast like figureheads. The boat was our one extravagance back then, and Nancy and I, while explaining why we couldn't afford to go to Disney World, would often point out that we weren't a Disney World family, we were a boat-owning family—a *wooden*-boat-owning family.

The person who really taught me how to get around in a boat was Chip. I spent hours sailing with him back in those early years, sometimes in his boat and sometimes in mine. He was a naturally gifted and graceful sailor, able to shift his weight so precisely while tacking—turning the boat across the wind—that the boat never stuttered or flapped coming around. Chip had a map in his head of the whole town: the beaches, the marshes, the hollows where wild asparagus grew, the fields where Indian arrowheads appeared in the spring, heaved up by the winter frosts. And his interior map of the river was more detailed than any chart. He knew where the tide ran fastest and slowest, the places where the current even turned back on itself in a little eddy. He knew how to get through the shallows, as he did on that afternoon when I was startled to see him sailing over to pick up his daughter. He knew where to find quahogs at low tide, feeling for them with your feet. His favorite spot was a shallow he called Hog Heaven, because the 'hogs were so abundant, and while there he'd sometimes eat a few right on the spot, smashing the hard shell on the boat's deck cleat. He knew the sandflats where you could beach a boat on a hot day and take a quick dip in a nearby pool of deep water, and he also knew all the spots to avoid: the Toilet, for example, an eddy by the harbor mouth where on the wrong tide you could find yourself flushed out to sea; and the Vacuum, a place near the shore where the wind invariably died. Once we were sailing when out of nowhere a fog blew in—not the kind of wispy, smoky fog that sometimes materializes at the end of an August afternoon, turning the landscape into a moody Whistler-like painting, but a sudden, dense blanket that rendered invisible even the bow of the boat we were sitting in. Had I been alone, I would have been scared shitless. After a couple of tacks I lost all sense of direction. But Chip, following some compass in his head, steered us safely home and had us on the mooring before I knew where we were—an astonishing feat of navigation. Even now, after decades on the river, I still turn tail at the first hint of fog.

Our sailing trips were mostly quiet, and when we did talk, it wasn't about anything profound. Occasionally he reminisced about the Coast Guard and how much he had enjoyed life at sea—keeping watch, shooting sun sights, plotting a course. A couple of times he brought up Vietnam but didn't go into much detail, except to say that his time there probably instilled a false confidence that he could get through anything. His wasn't an especially horrific war, I gathered, but he did get shot at a few times and had some friends who died there. I think he came home glad to be alive and determined to be happy, and that his wish to put the war behind him accounted for his unshakable sense of contentment and his habit of putting a positive spin on everything. If you asked him how his day or week had been, the answer was invariably "Great!" He talked fondly and gratefully about his ship's translator, Tien, whom he and a fellow officer helped bring to this country. (For a few days after he got here, Tien stayed with Chip and Gay, and even attended a charades party, where he put on a policeman's uniform. He probably thought dressing up like this was something Americans did all the time.)

But in general Chip was very good at not going deep or long on anything of a personal nature, and at not thinking about things he'd just as soon forget. It was as if he had inside him a vast cellar where he could shovel away all sorts of worries and bothers. I'm not much better. But in our defense, what was there to say when the whole point was simply to take in the beauty of where we were? The harbor, the busy lobster fleet, the river, with its marshes, its inlets, its farms rolling right down to the shore. Sometimes you could hear cattle lowing. At low tide we'd come across the shell-fishermen. There are still a few of these guys making a living from small boats, scalloping in winter, raking for quahogs in warmer weather. It's hard, backbreaking work, and they're not going to give you a big cheerful wave. Nod at them and if you're lucky, you might get a nod back. There were the birds—gulls everywhere; the cormorants loitering, shrug-shouldered, on rocks and pilings; and the egrets, which perch motionless in trees when they're not mincing through the shallows. In particular there was one big pine where they used to gather in such number that the branches seemed festooned with them, like the trees in front yards the night before Halloween after teenagers have been around hurling rolls of toilet paper. And always there was that never-wearying bit of magic—the common-sense-defying lift that enables a boat to sail almost into the wind. Once when we were sailing Chip turned to me and said, "You know, you can do this." He had a way sometimes of making jokes out of the obvious. After a good meal he might say, "You know, when you're hungry, the best thing you can eat is food." But this time he wasn't kidding, and he repeated himself: "You can *do* this." I think he meant it as an expression of wonder and gratitude.

Right now, our second Beetle—named *Loon*, by the way, after both the bird and the crazy person—is rolled over on one side and up on sawhorses in the barn just a few feet from the little room where I'm writing this. It looks like—well, a boat out of water, and I don't have to look too hard to see signs of its age: black spots on the coaming, places where the deck canvas is almost worn through, a worrisome spot near the bow where it looks like the stem piece is coming delaminated. If I wanted to be anthropomorphic, I could say it reminds me a little of myself. For years I had the boat maintained by the people who built it, the folks at Beetle, but now—out of cheapness and a sense that I can take better care of it than some unfeeling stranger—I do the work myself. Wooden boats require a fair amount of upkeep, which is probably the main reason they've mostly been replaced by fiberglass. The bottom and topsides need to be sanded, scraped, and painted every year; the brightwork and spars have to be sanded and varnished and then sanded and varnished again. I've heard of fanatics who insist on six or seven coats, but I draw the line at three—"good enough for government work," as my father used to say of something that was okay but not perfect. I've got all the boat work down now, and though I sometimes complain, it's work I enjoy. Also, it helps immeasurably that Nancy recently gave me a set of noise-canceling headphones, enabling me to listen to audiobooks while I work. I even listened to "Victory," one of Conrad's great sea stories, while sanding last spring, though most of the time my choices aren't so nautically appropriate. While doing the spars I listened to Len Deighton. The sanding part of me was in southeastern Massachusetts, while the rest was in Cold War Berlin.

Nowadays, with Chip gone, I do most of my sailing with Nancy, and we have it down to a wordless routine, a sort of couple's minuet. Before I even have the dinghy tied to the mooring float she's on board and is fitting the rudder onto the stern. This takes a certain amount of skill. The pintles—two metal pegs attached to the back of the rudder—have to be dropped into two circular pieces in the stern, the gudgeons, which can be hard to find when the boat is bobbing around. On the occasions when I sail alone I have trouble lining everything up and will often get the top pintle in while the bottom one dodges its receptacle, so that the rudder swings loose, like a broken shutter. But Nancy already has the tiller in place—passed through an opening in the stern and beneath two metal straps on the top of the rudder—by the time I climb on board and is starting to remove the cloth strips that tie the sail down. Without even looking back, I step toward the bow, undo the last sail tie, grab the two halyards—the ropes that raise the sail—and pull. Both hands tug together, until the right-hand line won't go any farther, so I quickly tie it off to the cleat on the deck in front. With the left hand now, I raise the gaff until the sail is setting nicely, and tie that line off too.

By now Nancy has the boom crutch out—the wooden piece that holds the boom in place when the sail is furled—and, ducking under the boom, I cast off the mooring line, giving a little tug to head the boat away from the wind. We're off! When I get back to my place in the cockpit, Nancy has trimmed the sheet and is pushing the tiller toward me.

She sits on the port side, and I'm on the starboard. I don't know why, exactly—that's just how we've been doing it for decades. We tack just by passing the tiller back and forth, and sometimes if the wind is right and we're headed to our favorite destination, a part of the river called the Let, it's a two-tack sail. I take us out through an opening in the marsh and around a rocky point that guards the opening to the Let—if I haul in the sheet and we get lucky with a little puff here, (come on, wind!) I can just make it—and on the way back she lets out the sail and we ride the wind home. The joy of all this never gets old for me—the flutter of the sail, the slap of the bow wave, the burbling of the wake, the tug on the tiller, the lift of the stern quarter as it catches a swell. It's like flying, in a way. And though we sometimes take the same route day after day, that never gets old either.

I used to sail on a big boat, back when I was friendly with a couple of older guys who owned a thirty-foot sloop that was a little too much for them and who were happy to have someone like me to grind winches, haul in the anchors and even, as I did a couple of times, ascend the mast in a bosun's chair to fix the wind indicator or retrieve an errant halyard. A lot of the challenge in those days was navigational—and since none of us was very good at plotting (or sticking to) a direct compass course, we tended to stumble from buoy to buoy, like a drunk making his way from the living room to the john, heading first for an end table, then grabbing the back of a nearby sofa before slanting toward the doorjamb and bouncing down the hall. It was thrilling when, off on the horizon, we saw where we were actually headed—the entrance to Menemsha Harbor, say, or the silhouette of Block Island. But I wouldn't trade any of our Beetle voyages to have those cruising days back again, and I find as much satisfaction now in little navigational challenges—working my way through this particular marsh or dealing with the tricky tide down by the bridge—as I did in my oceangoing days, when we just put the boat on a course and kept it there, paying more attention to the compass than to the wind and waves. Small-boat sailing is more sensual and immediate—sexy even. You're not in a hurry to get anywhere in particular, and you find yourself making haste slowly, not unlike the way summer itself does: nothing happens for a while, and there's nothing much to do except tweak the sheet now and then and feel the sun on your face, the breeze ruffling the back of your neck. And yet all the while the tide is changing, the clouds are moving, and you feel, in a way that you never do on land, that you're in touch with the basic motions of the planet itself as it spins its way around.

The other thing about sailing with Nancy: we have conversations. We talk about the children, the grand-children, about what's for supper. We talk sometimes about how lucky we are to be able to do this. I often find myself thinking of Chip then, and wondering what he would make of all our chatter. Back on the mooring it's the whole drill, the minuet in reverse. The rudder comes out while I'm still looping the mooring line around the bow cleat. Halyards uncleated, the sail slowly drops, the pulleys squeaking a little, and the boom is lifted back into its crutch. I furl the sail; Nancy deftly slips the tie strips around the bunched fabric and makes them fast. Shipshape. Back into the dinghy then, first Nancy in the stern, then me amid-ships. This is the tricky part, transferring unlimber middle-aged bodies from one small bobbing vessel to another, even smaller one, and may be our undoing one day, as it was for Chip when he could no longer swing his legs over the gunwale. But so far so good. I'm pulling on the oars now, and since my back is to the bow and my neck doesn't like to turn around, Nancy points with her hand to where we need to go. Home.

Buying In

Snowdie wasn't for everyone. We had friends from home come to visit who were distinctly underwhelmed and drove away baffled. My mother-in-law, too. When she came to visit the first time she was visibly disapproving, a disappointment to both Nancy and me, for my mother-in-law, too, was a summer person. She loved the season ardently and brought with her high hopes for it every year. She came from Maryland, and some of her most cherished memories were of summers at the family farm on Gibson Island, in the Chesapeake, where her father, whom she adored, was a well-known yachtsman and racer of Star boats. (He's someone I really wish I had known. Not only was he a great sailor, but he was also a legendary hockey player at St. Paul's School, in New Hampshire, back when hockey was just getting started in this country.) So my mother-in-law grew up doing all the things that we and our children did—sailing, swimming, beachcombing—but in a posher way. This was back when summering was still for the well-to-do. There were yacht club teas and yacht club dances. Dinner, even at home, was prepared by servants, and everyone dressed for it, the boys bathed and combed, my mother-in-law probably in a summer dress and with a ribbon in her hair.

She didn't cling to the past. For her class and generation, she was remarkably progressive. I sometimes wondered, though, whether her dislike of Snowdie didn't stem in part from the way it was a reminder of another, better time. Or maybe she just wanted a better mattress and some half-decent kitchen appliances. I do think she would like our present house, and not just because it contains some of her own furniture. It's nothing special. Chip, who had high architectural standards, and liked summer houses with big windows and sweeping views, rolled his eyes the first time he saw it, and I'm not sure he ever understood why we opted for a place so ordinary. If it had been up to him, he would have had us wait for years and years (while still renting Snowdie) until the perfect house came along.

Our son, after a recent visit with his family, sent us an email saying what a good time he'd had and thanking us for our foresight in purchasing the place. It was less foresight than happenstance, and, who knows, another place might have worked just as well. But this is the one we have. The house is a 1930s Cape. There's a big kitchen with a front window overlooking a garden; what our grandkids call the Fireplace Room—a sort of parlor, whose main focus is a hearth; and the Blue Room—formerly a garage and now a many-windowed living and dining space. A couple of downstairs bedrooms, a couple more up, reached by a perilously steep Cape Cod staircase, where I will probably break my neck one of these days, trying to descend in the dark. A basement with bad light and a noisy pump that grinds into action whenever you run the water (one of our daughter's friends once said the basement reminded him of a horror-movie torture chamber). All in all, decidedly modest, and yet I feel an enormous sense of good fortune owning it. I'm like my father in that way.

Some of the furniture is from Ikea, some we inherited from Nancy's parents; the rest is one step up from junk shop. There are a few nice paintings, and over the mantel a watercolor, painted by a friend and given to us by Chip and Gay, of Nancy and me sailing in our boat. Lots of books, some games, and, in the Blue Room, a big wooden dollhouse that nobody plays with anymore. Your basic summer-house odds and ends.

So what would my mother-in-law like? For one thing, the mattresses are all excellent, especially the one in the bedroom she would use. The appliances aren't top-of-the-line, exactly, but they all work: washer, dryer, even a dishwasher. She would approve, I'm pretty sure, of the pine-sided post-and-beam barn (a place that children seem to like to visit almost as much as I do) and of the big yard, almost two acres of lawn and trees and bramble. Not much of a view, but if you look down this little path, there's the river and (though you can't see them from here) the dock and our boats. She would certainly like that, and she would like above all the way that this has become a place our children and grandchildren love to visit. For my mother-in-law, family was practically a religion.

Poker games in the Fireplace Room. Bubble-blowing on the deck. Ice cubes down my back, which is how the grandchildren like to wake me in the morning. Croquet, badminton, bocce. As often as not, these lawn competitions end in tears, as one grandchild or another is convinced the game is rigged, the opponents cheating and conniving. They're like summer squalls, these weepy outbursts, soon over and forgotten. The shadows lengthen, the grass turns deep green in the afternoon light, and another summer's day goes into the books, entirely forgettable but also durably memorable, for its happy likeness to so many others. Here we all are, doing the same things we do every summer. These activities don't just pass the time; they also mark it, sweetly forestalling the inevitable hour of dusk—when pretty soon it's time for baths (more tears sometimes) and bed. Not a bad moment, while the bats are darting overhead, and the coals are glowing on the grill, for the grown-ups to sip something alcoholic and feel that pleasant summertime flush, that ethery, loose-limb sensation when, like a balloon, you could almost drift right up into the trees.

I'm not sure what prompted us to buy this place. We had talked for years about someday owning, instead of renting, but never did anything about it. Every place we heard about seemed to cost too much, and, besides, the drive up to our summer town from where we live in New Jersey can be brutal: hours and hours on Route I-95, a road under perpetual construction and subject to inexplicable traffic jams. I wasn't sure how often I wanted to make that ghastly trek, which seemed so arduous compared with just cruising up to the Camp. Even so, one late-winter afternoon Nancy and I drove up to Massachusetts, on a whim almost, to look at a house—a dump, as it turned out—that we had seen advertised on the Internet. The Realtor took us to see a second place, one we hadn't known about, and on the spot we knew. Love at first sight again—except that this was wintertime folly, not summer madness. In our eagerness we probably paid too much. I like to imagine that in a closet at the Realtor's there's a chart that special visitors are sometimes invited to examine. It shows the upticks and downturns of the real estate market for the past fifty years, with a big upward bump in the seventies, when vacation property around here became popular all of a sudden, and then a ski-slope falling off in 2008. At the very top of the chart, just before the line plunges down, is a spiky little peak marked with a blue star, like the top of a scraggly Christmas tree. "That's the McGrath purchase," the Realtor whispers, shaking her head in disbelief.

What was percolating in our heads was the notion that by owning a place we could extend summer, instead of just cramming it into a few frantic weeks. We had our first grandchild by then and wanted a summer place she and those to come could feel was theirs. It helped that I had left an editing job to become a full-time writer and didn't need to report to an office anymore. And something else that influenced our thinking—or mine, anyway—was that more than a decade earlier, at the height of our Snowdie days, Chip had gotten sick. In the winter of 1999, he found out he had prostate cancer. He was just fifty-seven. I'm not sure exactly how he learned this. From a routine physical presumably, and probably one long overdue. His combination of boundless optimism and determined repression made him avoid doctors and take his good health for granted. I seldom saw him sick. He never even got colds. But his cancer, when they found it, was pretty far along and of a particularly aggressive sort. His doctors told him that radiation or chemo would be pointless—the prostate had to come out. A prostate removal in those days was much messier and more invasive than it is now, and it took him a long time to recover. I drove up to spend a few days with him after the operation, and I was surprised by how weak he was. "I feel like I've been run over by a truck," he said. I was also surprised by how grateful he was for my having come to visit. He was emotional in a way that I had never seen before, and it made me a little uncomfortable. This was the part of our friendship that neither of us was very good at.

The first day we sat around and watched Monty Python movies. Chip was both tired and incontinent, embarrassed by how often he had to excuse himself for a bathroom visit. But after a few days he grew a little stronger, and we ventured out on short expeditions. We visited a guy on the Cape we'd heard about who had a "thermometer museum" in his basement—

a huge, random assortment of souvenir thermometers picked up from all over: Statue of Liberty thermometers, Eiffel Tower thermometers, Betty Boop and Pink Panther thermometers, you name it. We went to Newport, Rhode Island, and poked around in bookshops and visited a boatbuilding school there. We also drove out to Brenton Point, where one summer Chip had been a babysitter/companion for a rich kid who lived in one of the mansions. Another day we drove to Marion, Massachusetts, and, even though it was cold and gray, looked at a golf course I had heard about, a nine-holer dating back to 1904 and little changed. The bunkers were squarish, and on a couple of holes old stone walls guarded the greens, just as they do at Berwick in Scotland. It was like old times, our company effortless, and Chip mentioned his illness only once, when he said to me, "Pal, I hope this never happens to you." I hoped so, too, and in fact became a pain in the neck at my doctor's office, demanding a PSA test far more often than necessary.

After the surgery, Chip's cancer went into remission, and he seemed almost to forget what had happened, or, with that remarkable facility of his, to push it to a corner of his mind he seldom visited. But death, or the thought of it, began to weigh on me, adding a certain urgency to all our activities. I began to fret about my blood pressure and bought a little gadget that enabled me to check it obsessively.

So when we bought our house the idea that time might be running out was in the back of my mind. If we were going to put down roots, now was the moment. As it happened, a couple of months after we closed on our house, a routine scan discovered spots on Chip's hip and pelvis: the cancer had returned and spread to his bones. But it was all under control, he assured me. A little radiation and he'd be as good as new. I don't know whether he believed that or not. We went back to our old routines, only now there was more time for them, not just one overly busy month. There were weekends in the spring and fall, even an occasional trip up in the winter, when the landscape there acquires a particular kind of spare, clarifying beauty. The marsh grass turns brown, the dunes get scoured by the wind, and with the leaves down, you see vistas—sweeping views—normally hidden.

In a way, I began to think of summer as a year-round proposition, the way Chip did. And knowing there was more time took the seasonal sting away when the days began to get shorter and the nights colder. I still get a little blue, though, the weekend after Thanksgiving, when we shut down the house until spring. The late afternoon sky is often streaked a bruised purple then.

There's a long list of autumnal chores to be done. The gutters have to be cleaned, the lawn furniture put away, the pipes drained, the pump turned off, the chimney damper shut. I carefully change the oil and oil filter on the outboard and squirt sweet-smelling fogging oil in the cylinders, to keep them from gumming up in the cold. I take out the battery and bilge pump, coil all the lines, and stow everything so carefully that when spring arrives I can never remember where half of it is. The whole operation feels like a funeral.

Swimming

Swimming is probably the first thing people think about when they think about summer. It's the most basic and essential of all the summer experiences: just getting wet. If you can't make it to the beach, even a garden hose or an opened fire hydrant will do. We crave the coolness, the slipperiness, but we also soak ourselves because that's what you're supposed to do in summer. It's as if we are all participants in some dimly remembered ritual, the primal dunking.

I'm a terrible swimmer, clumsy and inefficient. I exhaust myself in just one lap of a pool. Once, in college, I almost drowned while swimming at Third Beach in Newport, Rhode Island. I was a little beered up, and the next thing I knew I was caught in a current pulling me out to sea. One of my friends had to haul me in, like a piece of driftwood.

My excuse is that I was never properly taught.

When I was a boy, I modeled myself after Buster Crabbe, Tarzan on TV, who swam with an exaggerated eggbeater-like arm motion. That swimming also entailed leg action—kicking—never occurred to me. And now it's too late. I can kick or I can stroke, but not both at once. In the part of my brain meant to synchronize arm and leg movement, the wires are down. I understand now that to breathe while swimming you're supposed to turn your head to one side or the other, over and over, snatching some air when your face comes out of the water, but I can't do that either. Mostly I just hold my breath for as long as I can and then panic and come up for a gasp.

If you think about it, swimming is a fairly unnatural activity, and it's amazing that people ever figured it out. How many aspiring swimmers drowned, I wonder, before someone finally got the knack? Benjamin Franklin, who championed the healthful benefits of swimming, also invented what may have been the first life jacket: a cork-lined waistcoat. There are mentions of swimming in classical antiquity, but it doesn't seem like something everyone knew how to do. Herodotus says, for example, that the reason the Greeks won the Battle of Salamis is that they were able to swim, while the Persians, who couldn't, all drowned. The great Roman historian Tacitus says that Caesar's legionnaires used to go swimming in their armor, which seems far-fetched. In England, recreational swimming didn't become popular until the nineteenth century, when "bathing machines" were introduced at seaside resorts. These were wagons in which you disrobed—and if you were a woman, put on a cumbersome swimming costume—and then were rolled out to sea. I suspect that most people then just dabbled in the water or, at best, attempted a brief doggy paddle. When Byron swam four miles across the Hellespont in 1810, it was heralded as a prodigious feat, which suggests that few people then were really strong swimmers. (Byron, by the way, probably swam the breaststroke. The crawl didn't come along until the 1920s.)

The Romantics often rhapsodized about swimming: they saw it as a way of connecting to the sublime. They also appreciated that swimming is one of the more sensual experiences we can have. Hopeless swimmer though I am, I like to dive in at night (sober) and float (close to shore). It's eerie and yet calming, that feeling of weightlessness, and I always leave the water feeling alive in my own skin.

Our kids used to enjoy night swimming too, especially when the bioluminescent plankton was abundant and by kicking and splashing they would make the water come alive with hundreds of little sparkles—fairy lights. And I remember one moonlit night when Nancy, Chip, Gay, and I all went skinny-dipping. I felt much less shy than I imagined I would, because without my glasses I'm practically blind. I didn't see nakedness, really, just some glowing white-ness, and I imagined that's all others could see of me. Mostly I was aware of the darkness, almost velvety, pinpricked with stars, and of how in the distance you couldn't tell where the water ended and the sky began. This wouldn't have been nearly so much fun in the daylight.

Watching the kids swim was more joyful than swimming on my own. I loved when they were still learning and would paddle frantically, their panting, upturned heads, seal-like, barely above the surface. My heart used to swell a little at their bravery and fragility. With every passing year, they became more intrepid, walked out deeper, braving bigger and bigger waves, until finally they were on their own and I let the lifeguards watch them. Now, the grandchildren are repeating the cycle. Sam, the youngest, after shedding his water wings began to delight more in the water than anyone I have ever known. Nate and Lizzie, our oldest grandchildren, have reached the stage where they're bored unless the red "Danger" flag is flying from the lifeguard stand. They brag about getting rolled by the high surf and scraped along the bottom.

To accommodate them, as well as Ian, Sam's older brother and daredevil-in-training, we have had to add other water activities to the repertoire. There's towing the kids from the sailboat, the way we learned from Chip. It amazes me how fast you can pull someone from wind power alone, and how little it seems to slow the boat. But sail power is nothing compared with an engine. A few years ago we got a wooden skiff with a 20-horse outboard, and to this we attach a long rope and an inner tube. A grandchild plops down on this—or, in the case of the older ones, attempts to stand up—while the boat, at full throttle, tears about, banking hard, crossing its own wake, snapping the tube around like the end of a whip. Already there has been lobbying for more speed, a bigger engine, or even two or three (Ian's favored option), but I am holding my ground.

When the kids get tired of tubing, there's jumping. Not from the big bridge. They do it off a lowish bridge—with barely enough headroom to allow a small boat to pass underneath—a couple of miles upstream from our place. Or else at the Jumping Rock—Ship Rock, to use its real name—an even shorter distance downstream. The Jumping Rock looks a little like a small ship and is big enough that bushes grow on top. You get there by skiff or by kayak, pull alongside, and scrabble up as if you were boarding a bigger vessel. At the bow of the ship is a little ledge, and from there you leap—whooping and leg-flailing optional—and then swim back and scrabble again.

I drive the boat on these excursions, and at the beach these days I mostly do a lot of watery standing around. I'm not alone. At the beach in summer what you mostly see is not swimming, strictly speaking, but bathing. We might as well be back in the nineteenth century. Out beyond where the waves break there might be a show-off slowly cruising back and forth, momentarily disappearing behind a swell and then rising back into view, arms and legs effortlessly churning through the sea. The kids are flinging themselves around, of course, or trying to catch a wave on a boogie board. But we grown-ups are mostly standing there, knee- to waist-deep, looking out to sea. When a wave comes along, we might jump up, or just let it break over us. I don't stay in for long. The older I get, the colder the ocean seems. My insulation seems to have worn thin.

Another thing: sitting on the beach has begun to drive me a little crazy. It's always so hot. I feel I'm baking some badly needed brain cells. So instead I like to walk along the beach, watching other people's grand-children, inspecting their trenches and sandcastles, and discreetly eyeing their parents. Tattoos every-where! They seem like standard beachwear these days. Often Nancy accompanies me. We'll walk the whole length of the beach, down to where the channel comes into the harbor, put down our towels, kick off our shoes, and plop ourselves in the current. This is more our speed now. We float on our backs. Nancy some-times keeps her sunglasses on. Depending on the tide, the water can move here quite fast, surging in or rac-ing out, carrying us along like pieces of flotsam while the shore slides past. On an outgoing tide, I sometimes imagine myself floating all the way to Portugal.

Golfing

Chip loved ceremony, games, and competition. He had ribbons and trophies for everything—for Wiffle Ball, horseshoes, even for beer-chugging. I especially cherished a silver-plated loving cup, picked up in a junk store, that he awarded every summer to the guy who had lost the most golf balls in a single round. Every winter, he celebrated Robert Burns's birthday wearing full regalia—kilt, sporran, dirk in the stocking—and recited by heart Burns's endless "Address to a Haggis." There would be real haggis, too, and he would actually eat some.

A year or two after we met, Chip introduced Akimbo into our summer routine. Akimbo was a lawn golfing game that had been invented by Chip's father and another teacher at Exeter. I don't think either of them was really a golfer. Akimbo was just something they did on summer evenings while waiting for the martinis to chill. The basic idea was that one player would stand with his left arm akimbo and his right holding a golf club like a cane while his opponent shot plastic golf balls at him. A body hit was a point, a bouncer off the head was worth two points, and a shot right through the akimbo hole was good for three. Chip resuscitated the game and then codified and elaborated on it. A ball that whizzed by one's ear he deemed a "Mariah" (as in "They Called the Wind . . ."). He also decreed that Akimbo should only be played with old, wooden-shafted clubs, of which he had several, plucked from the dump.

For a while, it was just Chip and I who played. Then he introduced the game to a few others, and the following summer he staged an Akimbo tournament, in which his gift for ceremony and mock formality found new expression. He invited a dozen or so couples, and everyone was asked to dress in white. The two Bens also wore white, with long green aprons, and before play began they gave the lawn—or "pitch," as Chip called it—a ceremonial trim with a couple of wooden-handled push mowers (also courtesy of the dump). Afterward, there was a ribbon ceremony and a group photograph, and some Pimm's, an old-fashioned British cocktail, was passed around. Chip agreed with me that it tasted terrible, but it was what the occasion required, he insisted. No beer out of cans.

The event was pure Chip—solemn and silly at the same time. He loved being ironic about customs and rituals, but I also think a part of him wished he could bring them back. A copy of that first Akimbo photograph hangs in our downstairs bathroom—men and women all in white, the winner and runner-up sitting in the center of the first row holding crossed wooden golf clubs. The image is reminiscent of a lawn party in Newport back when summer still belonged to the swells.

The Akimbo party lasted for several summers. Chip loved the occasion itself, but he also enjoyed all the practicing we did: just two guys whacking plastic golf balls at each other. I was the one who took this harmless pastime up another level by insisting that we try actual golf.

When I was twelve, my parents joined a nine-hole club near the Camp. It was an almost comical sort of place, with a par-5 third hole, for example, that made a complete U-turn; the green was exactly parallel to the tee and only about fifty yards away, but separated by a clump of woods you were supposed to go around. I don't know why someone never tried hitting a sideways tee shot with a lob wedge. For some of the members the main attraction was drinking. The bar was usually more crowded than the course, and the whole place was welcoming and convivial—a reminder that after the war, golf, just like boating, outgrew its aristocratic origins and opened itself up to the middle class. There were lots of little clubs like ours, and also munis—public courses—where you could just show up, pay a greens fee, and hack away. You didn't have to know what you were doing—and many people didn't.

Our club had a real pro, a leathery, whiskey-breathed guy named Phil, who spent a lot of time at the bar but nevertheless had the darkest suntan I've ever seen. I took a couple of lessons with him, and he taught me a grip—a pretty good one, actually—and just enough swing theory to fill me with confidence that I could do the rest on my own. Instead of taking more instruction, I pored over a paperback of *Five Lessons: The Modern Fundamentals of Golf,* by Ben Hogan, a classic manual that has been the ruin of many golfers. It took me years to discover that the Hogan swing, with its emphasis on pronation (whatever that is—I'm still not sure) and rapid unwinding of the hips only makes sense if you're Ben Hogan. For the rest of us, it works about as well as a car engine that has thrown a rod.

For a couple of years, golf became my obsession. Sometimes I played alone, sometimes with my brother. I went round and round those quirky nine holes, four, five, six times a day, baking in the sun. There was seldom a breeze, it seems to me now, and it was always so still that clouds of midges would float above the sixth fairway, undisturbed by even the most frantic cap-flapping. I would pound away at the ball with a swing I now recognize as classically over-the-top—that's to say, all wrong. I yearned to get better, and somehow persuaded myself that if I just spent enough hours out there, flailing away in the heat, improvement would naturally follow. And then, when I was sixteen, I gave the game up, turned my back on it. We had sold the Camp and no longer belonged to the club, but my defection was really political, or so I told myself: golf was too Republican. In truth, our club was mostly lower middle class, and I doubt there was more than a handful of genuine, card-carrying Republicans among its members. This was the sixties, you have to remember, and by *Republican* I suppose I meant grown-ups in general, or the Man, whoever he was. But politics was only an excuse; the real reason I gave up golf was I had come to hate it. I played most of the time in a blind rage—at myself, for not being better; at the game itself, for not being easier; and at whomever I was playing with. Most often this was Tom—younger than me, but bigger—and our matches became fraught in a way that would require a shrink to untangle. Once, as he walked ahead of me on the par-5 fifth, I unleashed an errant 3-wood that smacked him right in the ass. Left cheek, to be precise. It wasn't deliberate, exactly—he was nowhere near where I meant the shot to go—but neither did I wait long enough to make sure he was out of reasonable danger. Not wrongly, he accused me of hitting him "accidentally on purpose."

In recent years my brother and I have begun playing again, and I am mostly better behaved. I still do things like jingle my change or unfasten and refasten the Velcro flap on my golf glove when he is starting to putt, but that is just fraternal juju, something that goes with being part of a family. When I play now, I enjoy it. I've had some of my happiest moments out on a golf course somewhere. For this gift that has transformed the summers of my late middle age, I have a lot of people to thank: John Updike and Herbert Warren Wind, to start with, who on the page made golf seem more idyllic than toxic, something one might even want to try for oneself; also my friend and college classmate Jim Rogers, a superb golfer, who has encouraged me both by example (when I have trouble sleeping, instead of mentally replaying my own round, I sometimes picture shots of his) and by his patient acceptance of my early fumbling.

After Chip and I took up the sport together, the game insinuated itself like some kind of affliction, gradually intensifying, until it began to burn away time that we might have better devoted to something else. At first we had a rule that we would play only with used clubs, preferably ones from the dump (Chip's idea). I eventually acquired a set of hand-me-downs from my brother, and they were deemed acceptable, if not strictly dump-sourced. Golf shoes were unthinkable, a foppish affectation in our opinion, and for some reason remained taboo even after we had succumbed to the lure of decent equipment and bought real clubs that fitted us. We continued to make a point of wearing sneakers, and felt secretly superior whenever we saw someone changing into spikes in the parking lot. It was Chip who first broke the shoe barrier, picking up a pair of remaindered FootJoys at BJ's, a local discount place, though I had already backslid a little by starting to wear a golf glove. I don't know that it really did me any good—it was more like a fetish.

What did we think we were proving, playing golf in this half-assed way? We were like winos who tell themselves that swigging cheap muscatel doesn't really count as drinking, and I'm not sure we really foresaw how addictive golf would become. Partly we were just trying to save money. It was years before Chip bought a brand-new golf ball—there were too many lost ones waiting in the woods for him to find. I also think we didn't want to seem disloyal or unfaithful to sailing. And maybe we thought that by taking it only half-seriously we could make sure that golf continued to be fun instead of turning into the occasion for self-loathing that it was in my teenage years.

Though he was a very good athlete, who played hockey and soccer both in prep school and in college, Chip wasn't much of a golfer. He locked his knees backward, the exact opposite of what you're supposed to do, and because this kept him from turning his upper body in the classic, approved fashion, he had a wristy, windmill swing that took place in front of his body, sort of like a propeller. I don't know that mine was, or is, a whole lot better, though I've spent more time practicing and thinking about it than he ever did. Every now and then, when the sun is falling right, I will catch sight of my shadow on the grass as I take a practice swing and what I see there reminds me of some large piece of machinery—perhaps a person-sized version of that thing that shakes paint cans at the hardware store—in the process of flying apart.

Another way I think of my swing is to imagine one of those construction cranes you see erecting tall buildings and picture it trying to hit a golf ball. Your brain is the cab, up there at the top, with all the levers, joysticks, and foot pedals, and the tricky part is that it's not the same guy in the chair all the time working the controls. You're dependent on whichever operator the Imaginary Crane Workers Union decides to assign on any given day. Sometimes you get one who is smooth and fluid; more often he's twitchy and hungover, apt to go on mental walkabouts and forget what he's doing. Maybe because we came to the game late, and were low on the union's list, Chip and I often got this second kind, the crane worker who causes your club to lash out and strike six inches behind the ball, sending up a divot the size of a toupee, or else to lurch upward and just skim the top of the ball, squirting it off in an embarrassing little dribble.

On one of our earliest rounds, at Touisset, one of many funky nine-holers built on the stony, boggy, sandy land full of scrub pine and poison ivy that is part of the Massachusetts Bermuda Triangle, we were accompanied by our friend Bob Stegeman, a retired teacher who spent his summers in our town. Steggie or Steg, as he is called, made friends wherever he went. He was an inspired storyteller and had a warm, open nature that drew people in. He had been a three-sport captain in college, but he, too, was a lousy golfer—which Chip and I found very reassuring. On the first hole, I'm pretty sure all three of us dubbed our tee shots into a pond crusted with duckweed. On the third hole, I smacked my tee shot into the woods, where the ball loudly caromed off several trees. "That's a porn star, that shot," Chip said. "Plenty of wood." I have a vivid memory of the next hole, a par-4, with a giant boulder sticking up like a druidic dolmen to the right of the green. Steg hit a ferocious line drive that struck the boulder flush, and the ball came whizzing back so hard that he had to hurl himself to the ground in self-defense. On the seventh hole I swung from my heels, drubbing the ball into the ground where it skittered, like a wounded animal, into the bushes. Chip observed the swing, the shot, and the outcome and shook his head. He then addressed me in his best mock-formal voice: "Sir, that shot sucked so bad I can't bear to think about it. Would you do me the great favor of taking another?" Thus was born the "pitiosity"—sort of like a mulligan, a do-over for shots that were truly piteous but awarded in such a way that the offending golfer was actually doing his playing partner a favor. Over time the pitiosity became refined into a device, restricted to tee shots only, intended to make matches more competitive by preventing a player from taking himself out of the hole right at the start. All the other guy had to say was "Sir . . ." and you would happily oblige. And if, as sometimes happened, the do-over shot was even worse than the first, Chip had an invention for that, too: the gilligan, or the mulligan in reverse.

Why did we keep at it if our early efforts were so unpromising? For one thing, golf the way we played it was seldom painful—it was comical. We laughed ourselves silly. And not all our shots were bad. Every now and then we'd hit a good one—one that actually went where we intended— and as every golfer knows, that's all it takes to make you want to come back. In Updike's novel *Rabbit, Run,* there's a wonderful scene when Rabbit, who has never played golf before, goes out for a round with his minister, who is trying to talk Rabbit into going back to his wife, whom he has left for another woman. Rabbit tries to explain that there is just something missing from his life—some larger dimension, some sense of fulfillment—but can't define what it is until he steps up to the tee and hits a shot unlike any he has hit so far. It recedes along a line straight as a ruler edge, Updike writes, and just when Rabbit thinks it's going to drop, the ball makes an extra leap and "with a kind of visible sob takes a last bit of space before vanishing in falling." "That's *it*," Rabbit cries. "That's it."

What *it* is, is a glimpse of perfection, or near-perfection, something seldom afforded to us in ordinary life, and yet golf provides such moments all the time, or at least the hope of them. Your very next shot might find it—that magic inner harmony that allows you to swing smoothly and effortlessly, so that the ball flies off the clubface with a satisfying little click and then soars up, up, hanging there for a gravity-defying instant before dropping sweetly to the green. Moments like that lift you right out of yourself. And if you can do it once, you imagine, you can do it again. With every new round, the scorecard beckons, still unblemished, offering yet another chance to make up for past blunders. And there are other, lesser pleasures too: just being outside in all that greenness, especially in the early morning, the new-mown grass clinging wetly to your shoes as you stride along, happily about your task. Mark Twain famously called golf a good walk spoiled. Actually, it's a good walk with a purpose. The genius of the game was the nameless Scottish shepherd who invented the hole, creating a teleology for golf—a satisfying ending, or rather, eighteen of them. You finish a hole, enjoying the happy little cluck made by your ball when it finally drops into the cup, and then stride on to the next and the next, your steady, or unsteady, progress measured by the numbers mounting on your card—not too quickly, let's hope—until you hole out at the end and total them up. Good score or bad, you've accomplished something. Meanwhile, you've paid attention to your surroundings in a way you seldom do in life (unless maybe you're sailing), alert to the wind, to the blueness of the sky, to the cottony whiteness of the clouds scudding by, to the sponginess of the turf under your feet. Even when you're having a bad day, golf can make you unreasonably happy. I don't mind playing by myself, but even more I enjoy the company of others on the course, sharing in misery and in triumph. Most of all I enjoyed playing with Chip. I took the game much more seriously than he did, and eventually I became noticeably better. I liked to practice, for one thing, and he did not. But even so, it always seemed as if we were weirdly in sync. I felt his frustrations and occasional triumphs almost as keenly as my own.

Like Touisset, most of the courses we played in those early summers were built in the fifties or sixties and were squeezed onto old farmland. None of them were exceptional; a couple weren't in much better shape than my backyard. The prevailing characteristic was New England linearity. The holes tended to observe both ancient pasture boundaries (as often as not the out-of-bounds on the right or left was an overgrown, poison-ivy-covered stone wall) and the more recent demarcations created by creeping suburbanization. You were seldom more than a pitch shot away from someone's backyard or aboveground pool. The holes were foursquare, back and forth, and the hazards tended to be accidental. At Pine Valley, for example—the *other* Pine Valley, not the one in southern New Jersey, which is considered the best course in America—there was an enormous power-line tower in the middle of the first fairway, a sharp dogleg-left. The local rules said that if you hit it with your tee shot—something that happened far more often than you'd imagine—you had the option of either a do-over or playing the ball where it wound up. Chip unhesitatingly took the latter option when he once hit the leftmost strut of the tower with a loud whang and the ball took a huge carom to the left, winding up only yards from the green.

Without doubt, the worst course we played was the Bristol Golf Club, a forsaken nine-holer in Bristol, Rhode Island, not strictly part of the Massachusetts Bermuda Triangle, but close enough. Bristol was of a sublime badness. I'm told that the course was originally sort of rural-looking, and that Billy Andrade and Brad Faxon, Rhode Islanders who made it to the pro tour, grew up playing there, but it's now in the middle of an industrial park. The opening hole, a dinky par-3, is framed by a blue metal warehouse behind the green, and the last time I visited there was a guy out in front welding, spraying showers of sparks. The fifth, sixth, and seventh fairways used to be lined with what looked like old aircraft engines. There was an enormous crater in the middle of the sixth fairway with a diesel pump laboring to suck water out.

Aesthetically a notch above Bristol, my favorite of these nine-holers was Wampanoag, where some of Chip's ashes are scattered now. Swampanoag, as we called it, got its nickname for the obvious reason: the course, built on flat land along the Palmer River, doesn't drain very well, especially in the soggy expanse between the fourth and eighth fairways. I've seen golf carts get stuck up to their hubcaps there. Someone once told me that Swampanoag is where mosquito repellent was invented, and while that can't be true, during a rainy summer you would not want to visit Swampy without it. The course's other distinguishing feature was the clubhouse, which was built of cement blocks and resembled an antiaircraft bunker. Inside was a barroom, with old clubs and skis and hockey sticks on the wall; all the wooden surfaces had been varnished or shellacked so much that the place was like a time capsule preserved in amber. Even the guys sitting at the bar had a sort of museum-like quality—as if they'd been perched there for decades, nursing the same Seven-and-Seven. There was one guy who always claimed the stool nearest the door and was often hammered by nine or ten in the morning.

Why did I like the place so much? For one thing, I made a bunch of golf friends there. On days when Chip (who, unlike me, was not on vacation and had to go to work) couldn't sneak off for golf, I would sometimes go to Swampy by myself at six-thirty or seven in the morning, when I was often lucky enough to meet up with some other early birds. They were all retired—probably the age I am now, come to think of it, or even a little younger. Joe, Ralph, Ed—no, two Eds—and maybe a John. The Eds, in particular, were like truffle hounds when it came to finding stray golf balls in the woods. They seldom failed to finish a round with more ammo than they started with. I never knew their last names. One had been an electrician, one was a former plumber, and there was a guy who ran a garage. They were all living on Social Security and thought themselves blessed. They were well off enough to play golf a couple of times a week, maybe rent a place on the Cape for a week or two. They liked going out to dinner, but mostly to places with early-bird specials. They took me under their wing and offered lots of advice, not just about golf (their main recommendation was that I just needed to slow my swing down) but about life. They explained to me what was wrong with politicians—any politician, take your pick. And they offered that the differences between men and women were a mystery that could never be fathomed, so no point in trying. They sometimes played golf with their wives, and when they did, the men rode together in carts and the women likewise, a hole or two behind, with lots of waving and shouts of encouragement when they came within hailing distance of each other. They are probably all dead now, or have surely hung up their clubs, but they seemed a very happy and contented bunch to me. They felt they had lucked out in life and were proof of the American dream: work hard, retire, enjoy endless summers of golf.

The other reason I liked Swampy was that, more than the others, it had stretches that resembled a real golf course. Some of the holes were long and challenging. After a couple of summers of traipsing other courses throughout the triangle, Chip and I got so we could finish a round in under forty-five strokes, or better than a bogey a hole. We lulled ourselves into thinking we were golfers. The reckoning came one day when we played the New Bedford muni, the Whaling City Golf Course, popularly known as the Whale. This is an old Donald Ross track that's been allowed to slide a little. The budget is low, and there's a certain lackadaisical atmosphere about the place. When I played there a couple of years ago and asked what had happened to all the water stations I was told that the water was making people sick. Rather than trying to figure out the problem, they just took the water stations away. But the Whale still has the bones of a good and demanding course. It's long, with a number of lengthy carries over water or marshy brambles (grunkle, Chip called such stuff), and in those days some of the hazards were truly hazardous. The course is next to a landfill, which used to leak a little, so that certain areas, where runoff collected in orangey puddles, had to be roped off with yellow caution tape. What did we shoot? Don't ask, because I don't remember, but it was surely robust triple figures. It was hard to reach most of the greens in just two shots, and the greens themselves, domed and undulating, were a challenge to putt on. You could miss what looked like an easy one and find yourself with an even longer putt coming back. "I think at the Whale you need to know how to play golf," Chip said on the way home.

We determined to improve, and gradually we did, breaking 100 more often than not. That's when the addiction really kicked in. More than Chip, I became obsessed with becoming a decent player. I practiced, read books, subscribed to golf magazines, even took lessons. I got to the point where on a good day I could shoot in the low 80s. I also developed a small reputation as a golf writer and was paid, amazingly, to play in England, Scotland, Ireland, and even in China. Chip, who was less competitive than I was and cared less about posting a good score and more about having a good time, had a simple explanation for golf's vagaries. "The tide comes in," he liked to say, "and then the tide goes out."

I don't recall exactly when the marathons started, but it was long before Chip became ill. Originally it was just the two of us, and then we added our pal Steggie, who was instantly on board. The idea was to play as many holes as you could, on as many different nine-hole courses, in a single day—the Day of the Nines, Chip grandly titled it—usually sometime toward the end of June, when daylight lasted longer. Over the years the ritual grew more elaborate. There were trophies: a white patent leather belt, our version of the champions belt that in the nineteenth century was awarded to the winner of the British Open, and a hideous plaid sports coat that we presented to each other as if it were the green jacket at Augusta. Sadly, both of these precious garments were thrown out by spouses who mistook them for thrift-store junk. They were replaced by an old trophy left over from a 1950s bowling tournament. I still have it. And there was a champion's dinner, usually at an Outback Steakhouse but mistakenly held one year at a strip club that we thought served food. "Nah," the manager informed us after we sat down, our white golf shirts glowing weirdly in the ultraviolet light that illuminated the place. "There's just beer and naked women here."

But the basic plan remained the same, and was almost as much about logistics as about golf. We would get up before dawn, race to one of the Bermuda Triangle courses, and get in a quick nine while the sun was still coming up. Sometimes the place wouldn't even be open by the time we left and we'd leave our money in the scorecard box. Then on to the next course, and this is where it began to get complicated. We couldn't afford to wait or get behind dawdlers. We needed to play fast. This was before cell phones, but even if we'd had them, I'm not sure they would have done much good. At most of these courses no one ever answered the phone anyway, so there would have been no point in calling ahead. We'd spend a lot of time racing around the back roads of southeastern Massachusetts, our urgency growing as the day went on. Many of our courses had late-afternoon golf leagues, and it was crucial to get out before all those players began turning up. If we pulled into a parking lot and saw a bunch of pickup trucks already there, we knew we were cooked and would have to take to the road again. Some years our luck was so bad we only managed to get in four courses, thirty-six holes; more often it was five and forty-five; and on two memorable occasions we got in a full fifty-four, which is about as much golf as daylight allows for and, more important, about as much as the middle-aged body can tolerate.

The rule was you had to walk—no carts allowed—and if it was hot, which it always seemed to be, we were often worn out by lunchtime. One year I got dehydrated, or possibly fell into a temporary coma. I remember being unable to finish a spackle-like chicken salad sandwich and just staring at the same page in a golf course–maintenance magazine that had been left on the table. Something about new breakthroughs in pesticides. Chip and Steg were jabbering away in a language that must have been English but no longer made much sense to me. When I came to, chugging down some Gatorade, we were in the parking lot at the next course. "Did we already play Pine Valley?" I asked. Steg nodded. "How did I do?" Chip said, "You don't want to know."

My other memories of these outings are hazy, with one year, one course, blending with another and another, into an endless loop of endurance golf, hundreds and hundreds of shots. The bad ones I recall with more vividness than the good ones: a miserable plonker into the drink on the fifth at Hidden Hollow; a screamer into the woods on the sixth at Swampy; and a tragic stubbed putt on the eighth at Touisset, one of the few times in my life when I've had a chance at eagle, and I left the fifteen-footer two feet short. There was the year Steggie's body attacked him, as he put it. It must have been cramps, but he looked as if he were being grappled by an invisible wrestler. He was walking along the fairway when, suddenly, he fell to the ground. He got up and walked a few more paces, and his invisible assailant tackled him again. He finished the round without further incident, but with a crooked walk, as if his torso had been screwed onto his hips at the wrong angle.

A year or two later, there was the scourge of chafeage. I was spared, thank goodness, but in the sticky heat the two other guys began to feel their thighs and groin becoming raw and painful. By the time we got to the last course, Chip was walking bow-legged, like a cowboy, trying to keep his legs apart. I had seldom seen him in such discomfort, but he soldiered on and in fact began to play brilliantly and eventually came from behind to win the whole thing. He said later that it was because he was so busy feeling chafed that he forgot to think about his swing.

The marathon I remember best ended at Touisset—why does my least favorite of these courses loom so large in retrospect?—the final nine on a day when we got through a full fifty-four. The shadows were already long when we teed off. Chip plopped two into the pond and was awarded a rare double pitiosity. I sprayed one right, to where the mowers were parked, but somehow found it, and on we went. "It's a little like the death march at Bataan," Chip said. The air grew cool; the sun started to go down. When we got to the fifth tee I noticed bats darting overhead. By the time we made the loop of the big pasture that constitutes Nos. 6, 7, and 8, it was getting dark. When we finally got to the ninth tee, everything was quiet. We could barely see a thing, just the outlines of the trees up ahead, and there was a marvelous stillness to the air. This is what they mean by the "gloaming," I remember thinking.

Had it been any other round, we would surely have

quit, but how could we pack it in with just one more to go? We teed up and hit our drives, unable to see where they went, trying to judge by sound where they landed. No leaf-ripping or wood-thwacking—that was a pretty good sign. Miraculously we found all three balls in the fairway, and hit them again, in the direction of where we guessed the green might be. Finding them a second time proved a little harder, but there they all were, around the green more or less. Couple of chips, couple of putts, and we were done. The lights were on in the clubhouse, and there were people in there laughing and drinking beer, and for a second I was so happy and so tired I thought I might burst into tears.

What was the point, people used to ask, our wives especially. Why would you want to do something like that? Because we could, I guess. I think back on those days with great fondness, and like to count up how many collective strokes we made. Over the years it must have been thousands. It's a stretch now for me to play thirty-six holes in a single day. I can do it, but I'm so stiff afterward that I have to fold myself over like a carpenter's rule to get into the car. The Day of the Nines, a classic Chip invention, was partly a joke, but also a statement of sorts: that if you really like doing something—playing golf, spending time with friends—you should do more of it: too much is not enough. Actually, there is such a thing as too much golf. Sometimes for about a week after the Day of the Nines I couldn't even look at a club, but then the old hankering would kick in again, usually accompanied by a brand-new swing, though, this one promising to be the magic move—more wrist cock, hold the back-swing, weight on the balls of your feet—that would change everything.

Not long before Chip died I did something we both swore we'd never do. I joined a country club. Not a very fancy one, but a country club nonetheless, with a locker room, a dining room, and a pro shop with a real pro. When I told him, Chip looked at me with bewilderment. This was the ultimate betrayal of our plan not to take golf too seriously. He may also have realized that part of my motive was to prepare for a golfing life without him. I promised that as soon as he got his strength back we'd go over and play. "Sounds great," he said, but we both knew it would never happen, and after that I didn't mention the club again.

I go over there now a couple of times a week, and while I've made a number of friends, I sometimes will play by myself. I carry my bag and zip around, skipping holes if necessary to get ahead of any slow-moving groups I encounter. If I'm not held up, I can finish a round in three hours. The course is an old one, and until recently everyone thought it was designed by Donald Ross, a Scot who immigrated to America in 1899 and became sort of the Howard Johnson of golf course designers. His name is attached to hundreds of courses, some of which he may never have seen, and his holes have a characteristic look: raised, dome-like greens, deep bunkers, narrow fairways. Except that at my club those Donald Ross features weren't created by Donald Ross but instead by Willie Park, which is even better. Park, another Scot, was himself a far better golfer than Ross—after Old Tom Morris, probably the greatest of the nineteenth-century golfers—and he designed many fewer courses, all of them special.

I've grown attached to Park's track and probably know the terrain better—with all its quirks and undulations—than any other golf course I've played. You would think that such familiarity would foster better scores, but in my case, the reverse seems to be happening. My handicap has climbed about three points since I joined. Some of this decline can be attributed to age, I guess, though I probably drive the ball better—straighter, if not farther—than I used to. But too often the union sends me the wrong crane operator and his concentration wavers. I've started talking to myself on the course—not just expletives, but little pep talks about staying focused.

Where does my mind go during these little walk-abouts? I seem to notice things more—the clouds, the billowing shapes of the trees, a squirrel racing across the fairway. And sometimes, especially in the fall—my favorite time to play—I find myself thinking autumnal thoughts, remembering absent friends, Chip especially. I wonder how many holes I have left on my scorecard. John Updike played his last round with his son David in October 2008, and four months later he was dead. Chip's last round was in February 2013, two years before he died. We were in Orlando, Florida, playing one of the Disney courses, when a waterspout whirled past, and we never even finished the hole—the fourth. It blew so hard the rain came down sideways, and before we could race our golf cart back to the clubhouse we were sodden, right down to our underwear. We had whiskey and hot showers, but no more golf that day—or ever for Chip.

It's too gloomy to play every round as if it were your last, but the knowledge that your golfing days are dwindling lends a special sweetness to the middle-aged game. The good shots seem more precious. They linger in the mind. I have a whole mental file of them—big, booming drives, well-struck irons, long putts dropping in the hole. Right now I am picturing a sweetly struck 8-iron to the seventeenth, a medium-length par-3 with a slightly elevated tee and a pond in front of the green. The wind is blowing from the left, so I'm trying to draw the ball—bend it back from the right. The magic of golf is making good contact, and there's a saying in the game: "The hitter knows." The ball makes a special click. You feel it in your hands. That's what happens now. The ball takes off, soaring up and seeming to hang there against the sky before curving back ever so slightly and dropping gracefully to the green where it hops once, twice, and rolls to a gentle stop not far from the hole. There! As Rabbit would say, That's *it!*

Going to the Dump

Summer can sometimes give you the illusion that you've been freed from all responsibility. You don't have to work—at least for your annual two weeks, or however long your employer lets you off. Sleep as late as you want, or until the kids start jumping on the bed and demanding to go to the beach. Socks are optional, and forget neckties. Don't even pack one. You also don't have to shave if you don't feel like it. You're allowed to look like a bum.

And if you're renting a summer place, you don't have to worry about upkeep, about mowing the lawn, weeding the garden, or even about what happens to your garbage. That's someone else's job. When we were at Snowdie, Chip, calling himself Larry the Landlord on these occasions, would show up every Monday morning, load our plastic-bagged trash into his pickup, and haul it off to the dump. I used to like to accompany him—in hopes of coming upon more old wooden golf clubs—and now that I'm an actual home-owner, with a car-window sticker to prove it, I can go on my own. Going to the dump—unlike, say, dealing with fallen trees or a blocked-up septic system every few years—is an authentic summer pleasure.

Strictly speaking, the dump is now a waste-transfer facility, because nothing is dumped there perma-nently anymore. You sort your stuff—your garbage, your bottles and cans, your newspapers, your card-board, your clear and colored plastic, your batteries, your old computers, but not your busted air condi-tioners or discarded gypsum boards—into the appro-priate bins or dumpsters (one for colored plastic, one for clear, another for cardboard, and, right next to it, one for newspapers), which are then hauled away. In the old days, the place used to be a real dump— a landfill, I mean. You threw your refuse, unsorted, onto a giant pile and every now and then a bulldozer came around and tamped everything down, the way you press on your kitchen garbage can when you're too lazy to empty it. That pile grew and grew, though, like something in a fairy tale, and, now covered with long, waving grass, it looms unnaturally large, the highest point around for miles. They capped it off, I like to think, before it engulfed the entire town.

But everyone still calls the dump "the dump," and it's still a very satisfying place to visit. You have to stop your car or truck at a little hut, from which a cheerful woman emerges and, like St. Peter, punches your ticket before you can pass over into the realm beyond. I suppose someone more ardently environmental than I am could be depressed by the spectacle of so much waste, even though much of the stuff now gets recycled. I'm more impressed by the ritual of sorting and discarding. At home in New Jersey, we drag our trash barrels out to the sidewalk on Monday evening, and our recycling bins on Wednesday, and next morning they're all empty. The process is impersonal and more or less invisible, and it doesn't force me to think about what I or anyone else is throwing away. At the dump, on the other hand, you can't help feeling connected to your stuff and somewhat responsible for it. It's also fascinating to see what others get rid of. I like to imagine an archaeologist coming to our dump someday and trying to figure out what kind of civilization would abandon so much junk.

Here's just a partial list of what I've seen there over the years: two candlepin bowling balls, a sectional sofa, a badminton net, several umbrellas, a standing lamp, a desk, what might have been a church pew, a small refrigerator, a vacuum cleaner, a washing machine, a baby's crib, a bunch of wire coat hangers, a garden hose, an electric fan, a bicycle, a suitcase, a mattress, a pair of snowshoes, a beekeeper's hat, a pressure cooker, a skateboard, a bookcase, a fishing rod, a single ski pole, a pair of sneakers, a blender, a garden hoe, a stereo, some torn-up carpet, a set of Christmas lights, a snow tire, a hammock, a bunch of LPs, a recliner, a lacrosse stick, a couple of coffee mugs, an Exeter yearbook (Chip would have snatched that), and three motorcycle helmets.

I took one of the helmets home, because it was very cool-looking and I guessed, rightly, that our young grandsons might enjoy wearing it. A "pluck" is what Chip called something you rescued from the dump, and over the years my plucks have included a lava lamp, a light-up Halloween pumpkin, a model ship, a Mother Goose soup tureen, and a decoupaged milk can—all in mint, or near-mint, condition. I would probably pluck more often, if Nancy didn't discourage it. One of my most enduring dump memories is of a Sunday morning when I came across an old-fashioned push lawn mower and, thinking that you can never have too many of those, began putting it in the back of our station wagon. From the passenger seat, Nancy called out, "No way. Not another one," and a guy pulling his truck into the space next to mine turned to me and said, quietly, "They just don't get it, do they?"

On the other hand, Nancy used to enjoy tossing wine bottles into the bottle dumpster and watching them smash. (That was before they swung the dumpster sideways, so now you just drop your bottles—you don't hurl them.) She liked it even more than I did. She used a big, three-quarter-arm toss, grabbing the bottle by its neck, and got a lot of loft on her throws. I liked to go underhand, with a wrist flip, putting backspin on the bottle and causing it to fly end over end, like a field-goal attempt. Either way, there was something very satisfying about the launch, the descent, and then the crack and tinkle of shattering glass. We're taught to think of glass as something fragile and precious, never to be broken, and here we are at the dump just smashing the stuff with abandon. Thwock! Thwock! Pling! Crack! When you're done, you feel exhilarated, uplifted.

Sometimes I have an embarrassing number of bottles to toss, so many that I rush the job in the hope that no will notice. And so there's relief, too, when the back of the station wagon is empty, the evidence dispersed. I feel at the end of a dump run the way I used to feel when I was young and very religious and used to go to confession regularly. I'd come out of the darkened confession box and float down the aisle, my feet barely touching the floor. My soul was so clean, so shriven, that I felt I could almost see it, a gleaming capsule of whiteness. Going to the dump delivers that same sense of purgation. You drive in with your car laden: cardboard, newspaper, empty paint cans, the broken boom of a Sunfish sailboat, plastic plant containers, and all those bottles. You can hear them clinking there in the back. Then a few minutes of effort—lugging the trash bags and lifting them over the dumpster edge, dispatching the cardboard, flinging the clear and colored plastic into the proper bins, smashing the bottles, wham, blam—and suddenly the car is empty, cleansed of junk and detritus, and you, too, are lighter, freer. At least until tomorrow, when all that junk begins to pile up again.

Racing

Ring Lardner once wrote that watching a sailboat race was about as exciting as watching grass grow. He knew from experience, having been assigned to cover the 1920 America's Cup race in New York Harbor. The Cup races were big news back then. People went out on ferries to watch them and bet large sums on the outcome. It was a different time, before TV, and professional sports as we know them were just getting started. Sailboat racing—or yacht racing, we should say, because that's what the boats were; the private yachts of rich men, like Nancy's grandfather—also had a certain glamour. People still race today—even more than back then. The sport has become much more democratic, open to many more sizes and kinds of boats. But it's no longer much of a spectator attraction, unless you count the recent attempt to turn the America's Cup into a made-for-TV event, with catamarans that go almost as fast as cars and sailors wearing crash helmets because capsizing is so dangerous.

Sailboat races can be pretty boring, even when you're in one, but they can also be thrilling, a little hair-raising, especially at the start or rounding a mark, when boats are converging from different directions. I used to find racing nervous-making. Back on the Charles, I was timid and indifferent. I knew the rules, but little about strategy. Mostly, I was concerned about not crashing into another boat, and today that's still my great anxiety—that, or having someone crash into me. I still get anxious before a race, but back when I started racing the Beetle, a year or so after I met Chip, I was a wreck, fearful not just of damaging my precious boat but also of screwing up in public. Most of the people I was racing then had been doing it for years, and some of them, the ones I feared the most, were very judgmental, the kind of people who would sit on their boathouse porches and make fun of sailors who didn't trim their sails properly or who missed a mooring when trying to pick it up.

I didn't want to bring shame on myself, and I also didn't want to come in last. On my first race, with Nancy as crew, I did both. On the downwind leg, sailing next to another Beetle, worrying about a rock up ahead—a landmark in our harbor, marked with a beacon—I accidentally jibed and my boom went whanging into the other boat's side stays. I had, technically, crashed. Afterward I learned that I had been disqualified, because not only had I fouled the other boat, but I also hadn't made a 720-degree penalty turn. As a result, I came in dead last. I was so embarrassed that I thought I might never sail again. Why did I subject myself to this misery? Because of Chip's example. Racing Beetles had been hugely important to him as a young man, when he often took away some hardware, as he called winning a trophy. In middle age, it was still a matter of immense pride.

Racing also appealed to my own romanticized sense of myself. I was a sailor, by God, or wanted to be one, and racing was what really good sailors did. In time, I overcame some of my nervousness and even began to enjoy myself. In light air, with boats just drifting there, waiting not even for a puff, just a whisper of a breeze, sailboat racing is more maddening than Ring Lardner imagined. But in a decent wind racing is exhilarating, and sometimes just finishing, especially in a big fleet, over a demanding course, is tremendously satisfying. So far I have never taken home any hardware, though I did earn some software once— a ribbon—for finishing second. (It used to be pushpinned to my bulletin board at work, until it was lost somehow in an office move. I would give a lot to have it back.) More typically, I would finish halfway back in the fleet, which seemed appropriate for a guy with my skill set. I was far from being good, but at least I wasn't as bad as some.

I also raced once in the New England Beetle Cat Championship, an annual race held in different New England harbors. Most of the big Beetle fleets are on Cape Cod, which is where the really serious racing takes place. But in 1996, the seventy-fifth anniversary of the first Beetle, the championship took place outside Padanaram Harbor, a dozen miles from our town, and Chip and I sailed our boats over there. That proved to be the best part of the whole weekend. We left on Friday morning, right after breakfast, and tacked through the harbor and out into the ocean, where we caught a nice southwest breeze that carried us a couple of miles out, around a point where you can see the remains of a World War II fort—one of those places where people kept lookout for Nazi subs. The wind was so steady it was starboard tack the whole way, and I barely had to adjust the sheet. At one point I fashioned a self-steering rig, lashing the tiller over to keep the boat heading in the right direction, and lay down on the cockpit floor, resting my head on a couple of boat cushions, and read a chapter of *The*

Golden Bowl. I also drank a can of beer, ate a tuna-fish sandwich, and intermittently watched the clouds passing overhead. I don't know when I've ever felt so at peace, lilting along at sea, listening to the wake burble past the rudder. I began to fantasize that when the time came, this would be the way I'd go. Give everyone a hug on shore, pack a couple of tuna-fish sandwiches and a six-pack of Heinekens—what the heck, why not make it a case?—row out to the Beetle, and set it on a course for Europe.

By midafternoon, we were anchored in Padanaram, and that's when the idyll ended. There were dozens of Beetles already there, with more being unloaded from their trailers. We went into a tent and registered, and while we were walking around afterward Chip took me aside and said, "These guys are *serious.*" They were. A lot of them, we gathered, raced their Beetles *all the time,* trailering them up and down the Cape. Some of them even dry-sailed their boats—that is, they took them out of the water between races, so they wouldn't soak up too much water-weight or grow gunk on the hull. (How they solved the problem of shrinking and swelling I never figured out. The planks on a wooden boat shrink when the boat dries out of water and then gradually swell up again when the boat is launched. If I were to step out of my little office in the barn now and pay a visit to *Loon* up on sawhorses, I might be able to see through some of the seams. Next spring, I will have to fill the hull with water for a couple of days before it stops leaking.) Just the thought of stepping and unstepping the mast that many times tired me out. Unlike aluminum-masted, Marconi-rigged boats, Beetles are a pain in the neck to launch. The spars are heavy, and the system of pulleys and lines that raise and lower the gaff is confusing. The throat halyard, is that the one on the right or the left, and do you run it through its block from starboard to port, or port to starboard? Even after forty-some years I still screw up, though I have a well-worn diagram Chip once drew to help me. It shows a guy looking up at his mast and scratching his head.

Many of these serious Beetle sailors also had a couple of different sails—one for heavy air, one for light—and from talking to them Chip and I gathered they were masters of something we had never even heard of: tweaking the peak halyard—the rope that raises or lowers the top of the gaff—to adjust the shape of the sail while under way. Gay picked us up, and on the way home, where we would spend the night after leaving the boats in Padanaram, Chip and I spoke even less than usual. I don't know what he was thinking, but

I was already a basket case, worried, as usual, about making a fool of myself.

Like a lot of things you fret about in advance, a sailboat race—in my experience, anyway—often proves far more enjoyable than you anticipated. This regatta was far, far worse. The next morning the wind was blowing about fifteen knots, for one thing, or right at the limit of what a Beetle can comfortably handle, and the racing took place not in the harbor, as ours usually did (with maybe one quick dart out to sea and back), but in the ocean beyond the harbor mouth, where the seas were bigger than any I had ever experienced in a small boat. The fleet was huge by my standards, some fifty boats, many with the bright, candy-striped sails favored by yacht club–based Beetles, and the start was a madhouse. I was too worried about hitting someone to worry about strategy, and found myself in a jam right after the gun. I was on port tack—with the wind coming over the left side, that is—and the rules require that a boat on that course yield right of way to boats on starboard. I don't know who took it, but on our downstairs bathroom wall there's a photo that shows about a dozen boats bearing down on mine. I still remember the panic I felt, and the only thing I can compare it to is a terror-stricken drive when Nancy and I, newly married and living in England, tried to navigate the roundabout at the Marble Arch in London in our little Austin, with the steering wheel on the American side. The traffic there comes flying in about four lanes wide and if you're timid and uncertain, which we were, there's no help for you.

Nor was there much help for me in Padanaram. Trying to come about and get out of everyone's way, I got stalled by a wave and fouled another skipper, who began screaming at me. My crew was Ben, then nineteen, who until that day thought I knew what I was doing on a boat and has harbored doubts ever since. Somehow we got through that race, soaking wet by the end, and the next—this was a four-race regatta, with the winner determined by the best overall record—and, miraculously, we didn't finish last. Cold and drenched, Ben and I cut our losses and went home before the final two races, relieved to have survived. Chip, characteristically, stuck it out, together with his crew, his fourteen-year-old daughter Kate, getting through both afternoon races and finishing thirty-first overall. Respectable, and yet he, like me, was never tempted to try the championship again. The next day we trailered our boats home—the wind was blowing in the wrong direction for sailing them back—and after that confined our sailing and racing to our own harbor, where there were no gaff-tweaking hotshots, just ordinary sailors like ourselves.

The race that meant the most to Chip was the one held every Labor Day. It was the oldest of the local races, organized not by the yacht club but by some of the earliest summer folk in the area, among them Chip's extended family. The trophy, which the winner got to keep for a year, was a handsome half model of a Beetle with little brass plaques underneath on which all the winners' names were engraved, and the race had been going on for so long that, like the Stanley Cup in hockey, this trophy eventually had to be enlarged to make room for more names. Chip's is there several times, along with the names of some of his cousins. In the sixties and seventies he won fairly regularly, then not so often, then not at all. Why the victories stopped was a mystery to him. Sometimes it was bad luck: there was one year when after tacking back and forth in light air for close to an hour, he lost by about six inches. Sometimes he was out-sailed by younger guys. And sometimes he out-thought himself, a problem that was compounded when, after a few years, I became his crew. We decided to team up partly on the theory—a misguided one, as it turned out—that two brains were better than one, and partly just because my boat, cared for then by the Beetle people, sometimes needed to come out of the water by Labor Day.

Chip's great liability, if you can call it that, was that he knew the river so well. On the morning before the race we would huddle together and discuss what the tide would be doing at the start time. Incoming? Outgoing? How strong? Assuming a southwest wind, did we want to ply the inside or the outside of the main channel? An hour or so before the meeting at which the actual course would be announced, we would go out and take some trial runs, trying to determine which side of the main channel might be favored. We plotted—or rather, Chip did—every tack on all the possible routes.

Invariably, all this planning went awry. For one thing, we almost always got a poor start. The start of a sailboat race is actually something I'm pretty good at—schooled, perhaps, by all those years of fretting about crashes—and we talked every year about splitting the skipper's job, the way they used to in America's Cup races. I would do the pre-start stuff, get us over the line, and then he would take over. We never actually went through with it, though. At the last minute he was always reluctant to hand over the tiller, which made me even more reluctant to take it. He wasn't normally very assertive, but on a boat he liked to be in command. So after starting in the middle of the pack we needed to make up ground, and the way to do that, we always decided, was with local knowledge: shortcuts, eddies we could play, shallows we could risk. Sometimes it worked; more often than not it didn't. In retrospect, it seems clear that we should have worried less about tide and more about maintaining speed and keeping the boat going. On board, though, we would fall into the old trap and outsmart ourselves. We would have been better off just sailing by the seat of our pants.

One year I read something about laminar flow—how it might be possible to reduce the friction of a hull sliding through the water—and came up with a plan that amounted to greasing the hull of Chip's boat. I don't know whether this was legal or not, but it felt a little desperate. Before the race we actually drove the boat up on a marsh, careened it over on its side, and coated the bottom with Joy dishwashing liquid. Whether this made any difference I have no idea, but we felt pretty stupid watching a wake of suds trail out behind us. Perhaps the best race we ever had—at least while it lasted—was one that required no strategy at all: it blew so hard we didn't worry about the tide at all, just about keeping the boat upright. The wind was close to twenty knots that day—too strong, really, for a sensible Beetle race. Before the afternoon was over, one boat had retired with a broken mast. But we didn't even bother to reef, on the theory that this was the braver, manlier course. (Reefing is when you reduce the size of a sail by tying part of it off. That's what reef points—those little lines you sometimes see dangling about a third of the way up a sail—are for.) I have since learned that there is a physical limit, determined by a mathematical formula, to how fast a Beetle (or any non-planing boat, for that matter) can sail, and that in a heavy wind, piling on extra sail doesn't make any difference at all. In such conditions reefing is actually a good idea, since it reduces stress on the rig. Foolishly, though, Chip and I assumed that more sail meant more speed, and for a while our theory seemed borne out. We led at the start and at the first mark and were leaving boats way behind us when we eased the sheet and turned into the first downwind leg. The boat was already traveling at hull speed—as fast as it could go—and so the wind now, pressing with full force on the outstretched sail, began to push the bow down and under the water. Pretty soon the mast was awash and the sea was coming up over the deck and into the cockpit. We scurried to the back and hung our butts over the stern, thinking that might rebalance the boat, but it made little difference, and soon the boat was swamped, wallowing in the waves. Had there been a bucket on board, I think I might have been able to keep us going, but we had left the bucket behind, hoping to lighten the boat by an extra few ounces. (We would have been smarter forgoing lunch.) Sinking seemed a real possibility, or being subsumed by water, and for the first time in our ten- or fifteen-year history, we had to withdraw. We didn't finish at all. That race was won by two young women who had wisely shortened sail beforehand, outsmarting and outlasting everyone else. *Whistler,* Chip's boat, was never quite the same. She began to leak and creak.

I don't remember how we did in Chip's last Labor Day race, mostly because I never imagined it would be his last. After he got sick we missed a year, and then the following summer, when his boat didn't go in the water at all, and climbing in and out of a dinghy was difficult for him, sailing, let alone racing, seemed out of the question. Still, I had a crazy notion that on Labor Day I would drive my boat up onto the beach at the yacht club, where with some help he might be able to walk across the hard sand and climb in. But as the weeks went by that notion began to seem more and more far-fetched, and when Labor Day rolled around—too soon, as always, leaving me wondering where the summer had gone—we didn't even follow through on my last-ditch plan of watching the race from my skiff. Instead we stayed home, had a rum, and watched the Deutsche Bank golf tournament on TV. I was disappointed, and surely he was too, but in our typical fashion we never said anything, just sat there in front of the tube and complained about Rickie Fowler's outfit.

The year after Chip died, Gay and I raced together on Labor Day. It was a milestone for both of us. I was the usual basket case of nerves but tried not to show it, and she, I later learned, was anxious for a different reason. She was worried that without Chip telling her what to do, she'd be more a hindrance than a help. For a change we actually got an excellent start—perhaps ratifying, too late, the old notion that Chip and I should have split time at the helm, with me in charge at the beginning. We were first over the line, and second, by half a boat length, at the first mark. I remember Gay looking at me with an expression that said, I can't believe it! I couldn't, either, and as the race went on we fell back. We lost ground on the first downwind leg, when some boats came up behind us and stole the wind, and even more in the beat to the finish, when I made some dumb tacking decisions. We finished exactly in the middle, a small victory of sorts. I was relieved to have completed the course without disaster. Gay was delighted to discover that all those years of sailing with Chip had left her knowing much more than she thought. I run a looser ship than Chip did, and maybe that was a relief as well. I'm far less fussy, for example, about weight shifts. When you get to a certain age, it seems to me, you climb over the centerboard box as best you can, even if it's not graceful or right on time. We sailed home taking the exact route that Chip and I used to, through the twisting channel he called the Squiggle. Gay had been out here a couple of weeks earlier with her kids to dump some of his ashes, and now she took out a Baggie and sprinkled a few more. "Here you go, honey," she said. "It's me and your pal."

Lobstering

Lobster is one of the quintessential summer foods. You can eat lobster year-round, of course, but people rarely do. For a lot of New England vacationers, it's a summer ritual to wolf down a lobster roll or, even better, to visit one of those places where they pull a lobster from a boiling cauldron and then provide you with a bib, a hammer, and a few dissecting tools to eat it with. I know people who go about this task as if they were surgeons, intent on wresting every sweet morsel from the shell. They even suck the legs, and eat that disgusting green stuff from the thorax.

Lobsters are easier to catch in the summer, and that's probably why they've become a summer delicacy. Another, related reason is that lobster is expensive (I read a story recently about lobster huts charging thirty-four dollars for a lobster roll). For most of us, eating lobster is an occasion, not an everyday event, and one we save for the summer because it feels right for the moment, and maybe also because in the summer we don't mind having a meal that makes such a mess.

Early in his marriage, before he got a steady architecture job, Chip worked for a couple of seasons on an offshore lobster boat—the kind that goes out for several days at a time, working not individual pots but half-mile-long strings of them. He got to know all the local characters, guys with names like Crabshit, Jingleballs, Choggie, and Spaceshot, and though the work was hard and the pay lousy, he spoke of those days with great fondness. For years we used to talk idly about going out lobstering on our own. Regular fishing has no appeal for me at all. Every time I've tried I've been bored out of my skull, and, not coincidentally, I've seldom caught anything. But I learned from Chip the reliable satisfaction of shell-fishing, where you are almost certain to come home with a bucketful. He taught me how to dig for steamers, and how to wade around in the shallows and feel for quahogs with your feet. We did that all the time, and sometimes just threw them all back. Going after lobster seemed the next step up—one more activity to add to the list of summer stuff we did together.

Lobsters used to be so plentiful in New England

that you could walk out into the water and pick them up by hand, or else use a hook to yank them from their rocky hiding places. Because they were so easily obtainable—and maybe also because they looked so weird—lobsters used to be thought of as food for poor people. They were standard fare in prisons and insane asylums. To catch lobsters nowadays, though, you need a boat, and Chip and I lacked a suitable one. So nothing came of our lobstering plans until, for my sixtieth birthday, Nancy gave me a wooden skiff.

For more than a hundred years, skiffs—sturdy, flat-bottomed boats that can go almost anywhere—have been the inshore workhorses in New England. People used them for fishing, clamming, crabbing, gathering oysters and mussels. They can also drag for scallops, towing a couple of nets off the stern, and they're a sturdy platform for hauling lobster traps. Early skiffs were powered by sail or by oar and tended to have narrow sterns. With the advent of the outboard engine, the sterns got wider and lower and the run aft a little flatter, but the essential design has remained pretty much the same. They're workboats, solid and utilitarian. In the twentieth century there were two legendary skiff builders in our town—Fred Hart and Deacon Earle—and to this day a practiced observer can look at an old skiff and pick out the signature style of one or the other of them. Mine was built in the traditional fashion—planks of local white pine over oak frames—by a gifted younger builder, Scott Gifford. Scott loves sheer—that's the curve from the bow of a boat back to the stern—and my skiff has a lot: a very high bow sloping down to a somewhat shallow stern. I think he built it this way just for the hell of it—because he liked the look—but in practice it makes my skiff resemble a classic Maine lobster boat, with a sturdy bow for breasting rough seas and a low freeboard for ease in trap hauling.

Not that anyone would have mistaken Chip and me for real lobstermen. We knew next to nothing about lobsters, an ignorance perhaps partly forgivable, since no one seems to know very much. Professional lobstermen sometimes call lobsters "bugs," because with those long antennae, the rigid external skeleton, and multiple, jointed legs, they look like deep-sea insects. The earliest lobstermen thought so too. The name *lobster* probably comes from an Old English word meaning locust. Lobsters seem both prehistoric—which they really are, having shared the Jurassic ocean with ichthyosaurs and plesiosaurs—and oddly evolved. They are able, for example, to self-amputate a leg or either of those two big, asymmetric claws, one for crushing, one for pinching, and grow another. (The readiness with which they shed limbs suggests that they're pretty insensitive to pain, which is a comforting thing to remember when you're tossing one into a pot of boiling water.) Once or twice a year, lobsters also shed their existing shells and grow brand-new ones. Lobsters like the shelter of rocks and prefer water around fifty degrees. In our part of the world they tend to move offshore around mid-August, presumably in search of colder water. There's a theory that in winter they burrow into the sand and hibernate, but no one knows for sure. Lobsters can only swim backward, and then not very well, so they prefer to crawl around on the sea bottom. They move around mostly at night and, though they have eyes, find their food mostly by smell—that's what the antennae are for, and the tiny sensing hairs that line their undersides. They will eat almost anything—anything living or formerly living, that is, including each other and their own molted shells. A lobster's teeth are actually in its stomach—those toothy-looking things on the claws are for fighting and grabbing.

The lobster trap, or pot, as we know it was invented in the early nineteenth century, and the design, with two compartments or rooms—the kitchen and the parlor, as they're called—hasn't changed very much. The lobster enters the trap through a circular opening in the side, grabs some bait hanging in the kitchen, and then, following the path of least resistance, travels through a funnel-shaped net and lands in the parlor, from which it can't get out. Or that's the theory. A few years ago, some scientists from the University of Maine put a video camera down in a lobster trap and discovered many lobsters were moving in and out more or less as they pleased. The trap was less a trap than a cafeteria, in other words, and this may explain why, despite all predictions, Maine lobster harvests have been increasing in recent years. By putting so many traps out, lobstermen may actually be making it easier for lobsters to find food. If you think about it, they're almost like ranchers.

Lobster traps used to be made of wood, and early ones—the kind that sometimes turn up as restaurant decorations nowadays—had curved tops. No one I've talked to knows why. They must have been harder to build that way, and surely they were harder to stack. Flat tops were an improvement, but wooden traps were heavy and didn't last very long. In the midseventies, traps made of vinyl-coated wire began to appear, and though Chip and I had no idea at the time, the guy we bought our first traps from was one of the pioneers. His name was Bob Ketcham, and what I mainly remember from our first meeting is that he had an enormous lobster tattooed on his Popeye-sized forearm. It so impressed Chip and me that we vowed, if our venture was successful, to get lobster tattoos for ourselves—though maybe not quite so big, and not in so visible a place. Just where to conceal our tiny lobster tattoos became an ongoing debate, in fact—the butt? the instep? the inside of the wrist?—and it was our inability to decide, along with general wimpishness, that prevented us from ever following through. My son eventually gave us custom T-shirts with a logo that said "Double Chip Lobster Company," but cool as they were, T-shirts are no substitute for a tatt.

Bob Ketcham began making wire traps on the island of Cuttyhunk, but then moved the operation to New Bedford and by the time we met him was working out of a former schoolhouse, which added immeasurably to the romance of trap-buying. You walked up a flight of stairs, past several former classrooms filled with wire and rope, to what I imagined was the principal's office. Here Bob presided, behind a glass counter filled with knives and heavy-duty lobster gloves, while his wife, at a repurposed teacher's desk, did the paperwork. What Bob made of Chip and me I have no idea, but to his credit he displayed neither scorn nor amusement. He sold us ten traps—the legal limit for amateurs in Massachusetts—and showed us how to rig them with a line running up from the sub-merged trap to a buoy on the surface. He threw in for free some bait bags—little pouches of plastic mesh that you stuff with bait and hang in the trap's kitchen. "Good luck," he said as we were leaving—with pos-sibly a touch of irony, now that I think back on it.

Once you have some lobster traps, where do you put them? I tried asking some of the professionals but got the usual answer: I could tell you but then I'd have to kill you. Just like the guy at the fireworks store. One day I had the idea of following *Goose,* a local day boat from which the skipper sold lobsters right at the town dock. But the skipper either saw me trailing him or was just in a hurry to get offshore. As soon as *Goose* cleared the harbor mouth, the engine revved, a puff of black smoke shot from its stack, and within minutes it was out of sight.

"Think like a lobster," Chip said as we motored out with our first traps. They were stacked in the bow, and we had a bucket of semi-frozen pogies I was hacking into bait-sized chunks. "Rocks?" I said. So we headed for some big rocks fairly close to shore and, after stuff-ing in some bait, tossed the traps overboard. Traps go in with a very satisfying splash, and then you have to quickly remember to throw the line and buoy over-board as well. Otherwise, as we discovered, you wind up with a great, messy coil on the bottom of your boat, rope snaking around your ankles and threatening to haul you overboard.

Hedging our bets, we dropped the remaining five traps farther offshore, near where some other lobster buoys were floating. The guys who left them there, we figured, must have known what they were doing, though as the summer went on we never once saw anyone working these traps. It was as if they had migrated there on their own. For a couple of days we let our traps "soak," as lobstermen say, and then we went back out to check. We couldn't find them, not one. Chip loved to navigate, and ordinarily was good at it. He learned while in the Coast Guard and became particularly skilled at taking star and sun sights with a sextant and then working the mathematical calculations that give you a position. He was also good at taking bearings, using a compass to triangulate a position, and when we dropped off our traps he tried doing that, sighting all sorts of angles—to the harbor mouth, to a nearby navigational spindle, to the gabled roof of a beach club onshore—and copying them down, in his precise architect's handwriting, in a little notebook, which I still have, a relic of our folly. Careful as they were, Chip's calculations proved to be useless, probably because the skiff just bobbed around too much, and like drunks in a shopping mall parking lot who can't remember where they left the car, we found ourselves aimlessly wandering back and forth over several acres of sea. The ocean, it turns out, is a very big place, even a small sliver of it, and you can get lost even within sight of land. Nor are lobster buoys easy to spot from a small boat if there's any kind of sea running: one minute you're on top of a swell, and the next you're in a hollow. Lobstermen identify their buoys by color, and the one smart thing we did, purely by accident, was paint ours blue and Day-Glo orange, which made them a little easier to see.

Even so, we seldom managed to find all ten traps on a single outing, and every time we went back, they were seldom where we remembered. And there were other misadventures. Once I nearly went overboard. I was standing in the bow, scanning the ocean for traps, as usual, when a big swell hit us, sending me sprawling and halfway over the gunwale. Another time, I almost sank us. One of the traps had snagged on an underwater rock, apparently, and wouldn't budge when I pulled on the line. So I wrapped the line around a cleat at the stern of the boat and gunned the engine. Nothing happened. I gunned it some more and suddenly the stern began to descend, pulled down by the tautness of the line, and water began rushing over the gunwale.

"I think you should be heading into the waves when you try that," Chip pointed out. "Not a good idea for them to be breaking over the back of the boat."

By trial and error we learned, and even caught a few bugs. We were so excited by the first one that we high-fived each other and took selfies with the lobster held up like a trophy. The whole business of hauling and baiting we got down to a wordless routine. The guy at the bow would motion with his hands, directing the guy at the helm to where the traps were. Snagging one with a boat hook, he'd start hauling, hand over hand, while the stern man put the engine in neutral and hurried forward to help with the last, difficult bit—getting the trap up out of the water, over the gunwale, and into the boat. One guy would unspring the little bungee cord that held the trap shut while the other reached in and, careful not to get chomped, grabbed the bug from behind and extricated it. Or, more often, seeing an empty trap, he'd say, "Nada," and start rebaiting, stuffing a pogie head or two into the bait bag. With a heave and a splash, the reloaded trap then went back into the water, the line and the buoy trailing behind it like an afterthought. Some bugs we had to toss back, because they weren't big enough (there's a little gauge you use to measure them), but the keepers went into an orange Home Depot bucket. If they got noisy in there, scuttling around and fighting each other, Chip would lean over and yell, over the noise of the engine, "Hey, fellas, pipe down."

We did this for several years and I think about those mornings all the time now, even as I read stories about how the lobster fishery in our part of the world is dying out. Global warming, probably. It seems possible to me that future pals—the Chip and Chip of fifty years hence—will never know the fun of going after bugs: the freshness of dawn, the excitement of starting out, the companionship of shared purpose, the sense that anything could happen. They'll have to come up with something else to do.

From a practical point of view our lobstering was a crackpot enterprise. That first summer the guy who owns *Goose* was selling lobsters for a very reasonable $4.99 a pound. Taking into account bait, gas, a license, and the cost of the traps themselves, our haul probably worked out to about thirty or forty dollars a pound. Or maybe even more—I never wanted to do the math. It's safe to say our lobsters cost more than caviar, but of course they tasted better than store-bought lobsters. More mornings than not, we returned empty-handed. But catching anything wasn't really the point, though every time we did, hauling the trap up hand over hand, waiting suspensefully to see if anything was inside, and then spotting a scrabbling lobster, brandishing its claws, it felt like a gift. Lobsters are such strange, primitive creatures that just catching sight of one feels like a reward. Someone who really understood this was a Dutch painter named Willem Kalf, who has a painting in the National Gallery in London misleadingly titled *Still Life with Drinking-Horn*. There is a drinking horn in the picture, but the star of the painting is a lobster, a cooked one—bright red, and not greenish brown, the color of lobsters when you catch them—but depicted with such care and wonderment that it borders on awe. There's something almost regal about it.

The possibility of catching a lobster was really an excuse for what we called the commute—the journey out to our traps and back. Chip typically came by my place around six-thirty or so, or a little after dawn, and we'd put on our Grundens—the rubberized orange overalls real lobstermen wear—and head down to our dock, where he waited on a bench while I rowed out to the skiff, started the engine, and came in to pick him up. At that hour the sky was still red, and the boat covered in dew. The cormorants and egrets would be up already, making their matinal rounds, but the river was usually still, the tide seeming barely to move. It was often so quiet that when I fired up the engine, it seemed irreverent, like farting in church. As the sun came up, the river changed from molten silver to sparkling blue. We'd head out to the channel down the estuary, threading between two big landmark rocks, one of them the place where for generations the old-time summer people held a Labor Day picnic. The elders went out early to build a fire for chowder, Chip said, and, if it was chilly, fortified themselves with sherry. We used to talk about reviving the custom—only with rum, please, not sherry—but never did.

Then we'd shoot under the bridge, an occasional car thrumming overhead, and into the harbor, past the dock where the real lobstermen were tied up. Sometimes we'd get a whiff of coffee or bacon from one of the big yachts anchored in the harbor, and if anyone was up and about we'd give them the fisherman's wave—essentially, a nod and a raised index finger. If the tide was right we'd take a little shortcut, cutting between a marsh and the beach, and then out to the channel and into the ocean. It was always a thrill, somehow, to discover it there, so vast and various.

Some days there would be a swell running, or tidal chop in the harbor mouth, and sometimes it was as flat as a mill pond. I suppose you could say we were play-acting or, worse, doing on a lark what was for some people a real job. But we knew that—we weren't trying to fool anyone, except maybe ourselves.

Napping

This will be a short chapter, because naps are short. Strictly speaking, they don't have to be taken in summer, either. Gray afternoons in the winter are excellent nap times, and I still remember a fall quickie I snatched at a highway rest stop on a drizzly evening one September while raindrops spattered on the windshield. I thought I couldn't drive another inch, yet when I jolted myself awake with a half-snore about ten minutes later, it was as if I had been goosed with a Taser and I felt as if I could keep on all night. But for some reason—maybe just seasonal languor—I tend to steal some of my best snoozes during summer. I sometimes fall asleep at the beach, a hat pulled down over my eyes, and lately I have been retreating after lunch to a hammock the kids gave me for my birthday. It's under a big oak tree with a rope swing that was one of the first things we installed after moving in here, and if I look down a path we cleared through the woods I can just make out the river. There's usually a breeze, which causes the oak leaves to cast flickering shadows.

Napping is a little like drowning—if drowning were panic-free. You slip under, slowly and sensuously, and wait for the current to carry you off. Often it takes a while and random images flash on the inside of my eyelids, like a slideshow. I don't mean just those thready shapes that drift across your closed eyes sometimes—I think they're actually shadows cast upon your retina by floaters in your vitreous humor. I see actual pictures: golf holes, dead people, magazine ads, cars I have owned. Who knows why this junk clings to our brains, unless it's the stuff that dreams eventually get knit from.

Until he got sick, I don't think Chip ever took a nap in his life. He was too busy. But in the last couple of years of his life he napped a lot. I would often find him, midafternoon, asleep in his chair and would tiptoe away without waking him. I was kinder, in other words, than my grandkids, who once dumped me, sound asleep, from the hammock. I landed so hard and so awkwardly that my back was wrenched for a week. I sometimes wonder if he felt the way I do when napping—something I now do far more often than I used to. This is what dying must be like, I think—

a sweet slipping away. And if that's the case, then what is waking up but rebirth? You open your eyes and for a moment you're like an infant, all awareness, but without any clear idea of who and where you are. Then, like the tumblers of a lock clicking into place, the world begins to reassert itself: the knotted rope of the hammock, the sunshine dappling down through the leaves, an ant crawling across your leg. Time, which had temporarily paused, now starts up again, like a stopwatch. It's one-thirty on a breezy afternoon in July—no, August—and clouds are drifting overhead. Just as quickly, your consciousness starts to reassemble itself piece by piece: it's the twenty-first century in southeastern Massachusetts; you're you, the same person who dozed off twenty minutes ago. For a moment, the feeling you have—or that I have, anyway—is that same drifting, floating, opium-dream sensation you have on the first morning after school ends. Then you yawn and stretch and get up. You're back to life and your shoulder is sore from where you slept on it. The lawn needs to be mowed. The weeds around the stone wall need to be weed-whacked. The paint on the shutters is peeling. As Chip would say, Get busy, you knucklehead.

Dying

For people with prostate cancer as advanced as Chip's, doctors have a finite toolbox. When one treatment ceases to work, you go on to the next. Chip bought a few pretty good years this way, never talking much about what was happening to him. He may not have fully comprehended how sick he was. The first hint that he was worse than he knew came in the spring of 2011, during what proved to be the worst golf outing ever. For a couple of years Chip had been complaining of hip pain, and when it was especially bad he walked with an odd, swaying limp—like the Walter Brennan character on the old TV show *The Real McCoys,* I reminded him, and so he would sometimes talk in a Grandpappy Amos accent. Cortisone shots made him feel a lot better, and he got in the habit of scheduling one right before our annual golf trip so he'd be in peak form.

The trip that year was to Atlantic City with Steggie and another friend, Tom Winner—a neighbor of mine in New Jersey who by odd coincidence also spent his summers in our little Massachusetts town. AC was mostly an economic decision, because it meant that we could all drive there, but this trip proved to be an ill-fated one. We wound up staying in a tacky, golf-themed condo—tables with golf-club legs, golf cartoons in the bathrooms—in an out-of-the-way town whose name I have forgotten. All I remember is that there was only one restaurant, and it was also a liquor store. The golf courses, I should add, were not bad at all. The Atlantic City area enjoyed a golf-course boom in the early twenty-first century, when developers and speculators were still hoping the city would bounce back as a gambling resort, and the result, when the revival never happened, was a lot of first-class golf at very reasonable prices. As it turned out, though, Chip was unable to play. Cortisone shot notwithstanding, he found that it hurt him just to swing a club and even walking was difficult. He managed a few holes on our first morning, but pretty soon all he could do was putt. In the afternoon he just rode around in the cart.

The next day, out of deference to Chip, the rest of us decided not to play and drove around the Jersey Shore instead. We went to one of the casinos, where

I became so depressed that I could barely talk. (What makes Atlantic City so grim, I realized, is that many of those silent people yanking on the slots clearly can't afford to be there. Vegas is different—a cheerful town, not a desperate one.) We went and looked at the giant wooden elephant in the town of Margate, which is worth a peek, though I have no need ever to see it again. We drove up to Asbury Park, where one of those prepubescent beauty pageants was taking place. Everywhere you looked there were little clusters of JonBenét Ramseys. Chip concluded right then that he needed to go home.

The next morning he drove away—in what I now suspect was agony. He never let on how much pain he was in. The rest of us went ahead and played golf, at the Atlantic City Country Club, a linksy, old-school layout dating back to 1897, the kind of place I would normally love. But I was so upset that I played about as badly as I ever have. On one hole—the fifteenth, I think—I sprayed five straight balls into the water. I swore then that I was giving up golf—seriously, no more of this foolishness—and I actually kept my vow for almost three weeks.

The reason the cortisone didn't work, Chip discovered when he saw his doctor, was that his hip wasn't just inflamed, it was broken. The cancer had apparently eaten away at the bone until it crumbled. In early June he went to Mass General to have the hip replaced, but when the surgeon cut into him he discovered that the whole hip socket was rotten and infected. He sewed Chip back up—or partly up. He left the wound open a little so it could drain, which it did for weeks—a river of gunk.

Nancy and I went to see Chip a few days after the operation. I remember the date, June 18, the day the Boston Bruins celebrated their Stanley Cup victory with a duck-boat parade through town. Knowing traffic would be tied up, we parked in Quincy and took the T into the city. By 11:00 a.m., the trains were already jammed with revelers, most in Bruins gear, laughing and shouting. I caught the eye of a woman at least my age, wearing a heavy wool Bruins sweater—an antique, with the fuzzy bear on the front, not the spoked *B*. She grinned loopily at me, and I realized she was completely sloshed.

Chip's hospital room was on a high floor, far above the noise of the parade, though you could look down and see the duck boats, and it was a world apart. Chip was in great pain. At one point we heard him screaming when some orderlies helped him out of bed. He was also out of it. He recognized Nancy and me—barely—but had no sense of where he was. At one point he said to me he thought it might be some sort of seraglio—not that far-fetched, I guess, if you consider that there were a lot of beds and a lot of women hovering about. He was listless and blank-eyed and was slurring his words—the effect of all his medication. He could barely feed himself. Getting dressed or moving around except in a wheelchair was out of the question. It wasn't clear to me that he would ever recover.

We stayed for half an hour or so and then headed home. The whole experience had been worse than I imagined. Terrible and terrifying. In the car I began to get angry with myself. What sort of friend are you? I thought. If you cared about him half as much as you say, you would turn around right now, head back to the hospital, and smother him with a pillow. That's how miserable he was, and I couldn't imagine anything worse than leaving him there in his suffering and delirium.

But it was just as well that I didn't smother him, because gradually he got a little better. After a couple of weeks, he was moved to a rehabilitation center in Cambridge, where he spent weeks on IV antibiotics. I visited Chip there, too, and my most vivid recollection is of a guy with a dent in his head wandering around and shouting, "All I want is a piece of cheese.

Is it too much to ask for a piece of fucking cheese?" While Chip and I were talking once, a psychologist came by and said she needed him to answer a questionnaire. Was he depressed? she wanted to know. Of course he's depressed, I wanted to say. Why wouldn't he be? Amazingly, Chip said that he wasn't depressed at all; he felt fine. And when she asked if he ever had suicidal thoughts, he looked at her in amazement and said no, of course not. Was he being polite, trying to say the right thing? Or was it those mighty powers of denial kicking in? He spoke very softly and with almost no affect at all. He still couldn't walk and it wasn't clear to me that he ever would again. He had surgery again in September, but the infection was still there, so the surgeon just took out his hip and sewed him back up again. His leg was now attached to him by just skin and muscle.

Then he came home, back to his beloved summer town. Because he could no longer use the stairs, Gay had arranged for a hospital bed to be set up in the downstairs room that used to be his office, where he kept all his yearbooks and team photographs from college and prep school days. She also rented a big recliner—so big and overstuffed it was almost a parody of a chair—and that's where Chip spent most of his time, watching TV. ESPN usually, often with the sound off, but for some reason he also developed a fondness for food shows, the kind where people eat weird stuff. The wound in his hip, still partly open, was attached by a plastic tube to a little device that sucked out the drainage. He called it his bilge pump.

I didn't think it was much of a life, but he never complained. I got in the habit of dropping by every morning, on my way back from buying the paper, and again in the late afternoon. Sometimes he'd be asleep in his chair, and if he was, I'd slip away, trying not to wake him when I shut the door. Other days, when he was more alert, we'd have a rum-and-tonic and watch golf on TV. We talked, of course, but not about anything important. Day to day, little changed. But outside, the shadows were growing longer. The days, too, were getting shorter. Another summer was ticking away.

And then, miraculously, Chip grew stronger. His hip wound healed and he no longer needed the bilge pump. That fall, he went back into the hospital and the surgeon opened him up again and installed an artificial hip. Another, brief stint in rehab and he was home again. "Good as new!" he said. Not really, but not so bad, all things considered. Better, certainly, than I ever imagined, and I was again glad that I hadn't smothered him with the pillow.

We resumed our old routines, and even made a golf

trip to Florida. We made dump runs, went out in the boat and worked the traps. On the occasions I found myself thinking that Chip was living on borrowed time, I quickly banished the thought. That summer flew by even faster than usual, because Chip was back and I was blessedly happy to be in his company. In the fall, his daughter Kate got married and Chip, in full Scottish regalia, was able to walk her down the aisle.

The next spring, I again went to visit Chip at home. He was sitting in his armchair by the window. The morning was chilly enough for there to be a fire in the woodstove. Turned over in his lap was one of Michael Connolly's mystery novels. I can still picture that moment. The clouds are swooping by outside. The heat fan on the stove is whirring softly. We talk about the weather, the prospects for the Red Sox, and out of the blue, as if from another conversation, he says, "I think the monster has awakened."

"How do you know?" I say, stupidly.

"Just a feeling."

After that morning, nothing was the same. Chip's health deteriorated rapidly. He started using a cane, then a walker. The doctors said that the tool kit was empty. There was nothing they could do except help him manage the pain.

Stage by stage, I watched my friend decline. My

greatest regret is that we never talked about what was happening. I never asked if he thought about dying, whether he was frightened. I never told him how much he and our friendship meant to me. I was reluctant to bring up such awkward subjects. Call it cowardice if you want, but my sense was that he didn't want to talk about death or friendship either. I thought it was enough that we were just there in the same room.

I remember Thanksgiving after Chip got the bad news. Nancy and I and our daughter and her family had driven up to spend the holiday at the Massachusetts house. We had dinner in the late afternoon and a little after sunset Gay and Chip came by for dessert. We sat around afterward, Chip and I nursing a glass of single malt, and he began telling our grandkids a story. They were sitting on the sofa in the Blue Room and he was on the floor—why didn't we offer him a chair!—with his back to the window. The story was about two river rats, named Jack and Louie, who lived under one of the boathouses at the harbor and one day got up on the fireplace mantel and managed to lower a scale model of a Beetle that was perched there. They took it out on the river and sailed down to the boatyard and then back to the boathouse, where they hoisted the Beetle, still dripping, back to its place on the mantel. He had the plot all worked out in his head, and told the story in very precise detail. I've since learned from Kate that he had a whole repertoire of Jack and Louie stories, which he would tell her at bedtime. In other installments, they stole daffodils from a garden, erected a zip line from the tower near the harbor mouth, and hopped a truck to the dump. In retrospect, I suspect that he chose that Beetle story because Jack and Louie were stand-ins for the two of us, and that their journey was inspired by our own misadventures. But what struck me at the time was just how unself-conscious he was, lost in the story, and how much pleasure he took in telling it all, how much the grandkids enjoyed it. Often they were bored and fidgety after a family dinner—when they weren't clamoring for extra dessert, that is—but they sat there, practically motionless, for the whole half hour it took Jack and Louie to sail back to the boathouse and get the Beetle up on the mantel again before anyone could notice. It was an extraordinary performance on Chip's part. The inventiveness was no surprise, but I had never known him to hold forth like this. I think the illness had made him both less shy and more generous.

I learned later that when one of Chip's caregivers volunteered to tell him how much time he had left, he said he didn't want to know. It's possible he was in denial right to the end—that he couldn't, or wouldn't, admit to himself that he was dying. A little piece of paper Kate came across after he died suggests, though, that toward the very end he had begun tidying up. The writing is scrawled and almost illegible, not at all like his usual architect's hand, so clear and precise it could almost be print, and what seems to be a list of annual boat chores unravels into a series of wandering, muddled thoughts:

> spring work
> rigging, sanding
> mooring, dinghy, sticker
> getting ready to sail
> snaking the mooring
> evaluating wind, tide
> putting the boat away for the winter
> racing/sailing

When I saw this list it filled me with sadness—to see Chip in such decline but also clinging to things he had loved. What if some part of him wanted to talk about getting ready to die? This is what gnaws at me in the middle of the night, when I wake, as I often do these days, and fret about my own mortality. I wish we had had the conversation—for my own sake, if not for his.

Dying

Of his last summer I have two main memories. One is our final lobster trip, in late June. By then Chip was having trouble walking, and getting into the boat was a bit of an ordeal. Instead of stepping in, he had to sit on the dock and scoot over, sliding on his butt. He sat on a special cushion, taking some of the pressure off his bad hip. And he was no longer strong enough to do any hauling. He used the boat hook while seated and once he had snagged a buoy, he held it out to me, and then I grabbed the line and carried it back to the stern and started yanking. He was in pain much of the time we were on the water, but he never complained. He only apologized for not being more help.

Toward the end of his life, Chip did a lot of things unquestioningly—because they were the things he had always done and he didn't see any point in stopping. I sometimes wondered, watching him up there at the bow, whether he was as aware of the summer slipping by, and of how every time we went out, it might be the last. In my head, I was always counting down. But I was doing that even before the monster came back. I was grateful for his company. I would sometimes catch him wincing if the boat was pounding a little, as it tended to do in a chop, but often there was on his face a look of sleepy contentment. He was outside, on the water, where he loved to be.

On that final trip, after a long dry spell, we caught a bug. I'd like to say it was an angry, clawing five-pounder, but it wasn't. It was a runt, barely legal. Normally, I would have flung it overboard, but I was listening to that clock inside my head. I tossed it in the bucket and declared it a keeper.

A few days before the Fourth we made our last fireworks run. Thinking it might cheer him up, I suggested we make a detour to Exeter, New Hampshire, where he had grown up. We took a quick spin through the campus of Exeter, where he had gone to school and where his father had taught, and then he directed me to his old neighborhood. It was a development when his family moved in—brand-new houses within a prep school teacher's budget—but now, sixty years later, the twisting streets were green and leafy, and the houses, colonials mostly, looked tidy and well cared for. Chip brightened as we drove around, and he opened up for a brief spell, remembering the gang of kids who once lived there, all newly arrived, all more or less the same age. He spoke about digging holes in a vacant lot and building forts in the woods and lighting fires there. He talked about their riding bikes and playing Wiffle Ball and roaming around aimlessly, the way we did in summers back then, when there were no play-dates, no karate lessons, no adult supervision of any kind, and your mom just wanted you out of the house until it was time for supper. I was a little surprised by how small Chip's house looked, but that was nothing like the shock I had when, on the way home, we also made a detour to my old neighborhood in Brighton. In many ways the place seemed more prosperous than when I lived there. Brighton Center, the commercial part, with a bank, a movie theater, a supermarket, and a five-and-dime, had undergone gentrification. There were ethnic restaurants and groceries where before there had been only bars, dozens of them. Even my own street, Nottinghill Road, seemed spiffier—except for our old house, which had been clad in ill-fitting aluminum siding. I've since learned from my brother that it sold not long ago for over a million dollars. My parents would be stunned. All the same, it reminded me of a baked potato wrapped in foil. The upstairs porch, probably the nicest feature of the house, had been closed in and turned into a room, which had the effect of making the whole place look both tiny and crammed. How did we all live there? I couldn't imagine, except to conclude that as we get older, every-thing seems smaller than we remember.

Or almost everything. Not fireworks. We lit them off that year down on the dock: a Bada Bing, Bada Boom, a Motherload—both big boxes—and a smaller round canister called something like the Patriotic Salute. There was that never-worn-out thrill when the fuse begins to glow and sputter, a quick dash back up the gangway, and the anxious moment of suspense before the first rocket goes off. Has the fuse gone out? Whomp! Never mind. Trailing sparks, the first rocket went up, up, higher than seemed possible. It paused in midair, then a boom, and the sky was lit up with a giant blue chrysanthemum. (Only recently did I notice how many fireworks take the shape of flowers: mums, peonies, budding willow branches.) The sparks drifted down toward the water, casting a reflection, and then another rocket, and another, and another, flew up—a barrage, crackling and banging, until the sky was a sparkling fountain, a waterfall. Then quiet, stillness, a pattering of applause from family and friends watching from the shore. I beamed as I collected the empty boxes, picked up some blown-off wrappings, and headed back up the gangway, where Chip was waiting.

"Pretty good," I said.

"Next year we gotta do more," he said, but of course there was no next year. I'm not the first person to say that fireworks are a lot like life. They're great while they last, but they don't last very long. A flash, a bang, and then silence, darkness, a few shreds of burned cardboard scattered on the grass and a puff of blue-gray smoke uncoiling in front of you, with that brimstone smell. What fireworks are really about, I now think, is brevity, impermanence, the ever-present possibility of failure—the certainty, sooner or later, of a dud.

Toward the end of that summer, Chip's cancer had spread everywhere. A side effect was that he also came down with Bell's palsy. Part of his face collapsed, so that one eye drooped. His speech became a little slurred, and it was difficult for him to eat. He spent more and more time sleeping, and when he was awake he was often attached to an oxygen hose. A hospice worker came by in the evenings and sometimes squirted a little morphine under his tongue. To make him less anxious, she said.

Shortly before Christmas, Nancy and I drove up to see him for what I guessed might be the last time. We had a nice dinner, though he didn't eat much of it, and finished with a dram of Balvenie, his favorite single malt Scotch. Then he excused himself and asked for help getting to bed—a process that had by now become complicated and time-consuming.

What kind of Christmas present do you give someone who is dying? I thought about a book. Or a DVD. But then I figured he'd never look at either. So I gave him a letter instead. I told him—for the first time, really—how much our friendship had meant to me, and reminded him of all the fun we had had. I said he was what Romantics used to call a *genius loci*—the spirit of a place, its embodiment in a person. I wrote down things I had been wanting to say for years, and ended by saying that our summers together had been a tremendous, unlooked-for gift. I think now it may all have been a mistake—it was too late. And possibly I said too little. This book is what I should have given him.

He died in January, not in summer—that would have been too cruel—but in the middle of one of the coldest winters anyone could remember. The phone call came at seven in the morning. Nancy answered. When she looked at me, I knew instantly what it was and began to sob—the first time I'd wept in I don't know how long. But now I was crying not just for my friend but for myself, left without him.

A week or so later there was a memorial. By then, there were a couple of feet of snow on the ground and the river was frozen enough to walk on—for about ten feet, until I fell in. In my haste to scramble out, I did something to my leg that left me limping for weeks. The service was at the Methodist church, a white clapboard building near the harbor. So many people came—friends, relatives, colleagues, neighbors, former clients, people he had been on boards with—that the church couldn't hold them all. The overflow had to watch on closed-circuit TV in the parish hall—the same place where we'd met him and Gay so many years ago at our first square dance. I was asked to give one of the eulogies, and I said more or less what I said in my letter, adding that of his many abilities, Chip's greatest talent was for friendship. The proof of that was all the people sitting there, most of whom felt about him exactly as I did. For a guy who never said all that much, Chip managed to turn out an entire town. The best part of the service, as far as I was concerned, was a bagpiper in full rig—kilt, sporran, long stockings. Chip would have loved that.

That August, our sons and some of the guys Chip used to play golf with had another ceremony for Chip at Swampanoag. We all teed off on what used to be the first hole, Chip's favorite because it was so wide open and inviting. We played up to the green, and when we all got there I sprinkled some of his ashes in the big sand trap on the right, where Chip had spent a great deal of time when he was alive. He seldom failed to beach himself in that spot, and generally took a couple of tries to get out. I had brought along a bottle of Balvenie, so we all had a little swig, and then we went home, not knowing what else to do with the day.

A week or so later, the three of us who had been on that ill-fated Atlantic City trip—Steg, Tom Winner, and I—decided to play not just a hole but an entire round in Chip's honor. We drove to Sun Valley, another favorite course of his, one that had always been living on borrowed time, with hardly an improvement to the place since it opened in the 1950s. The clubhouse roof sagged, and the entrance drive used to be lined with abandoned farm machinery. But now, except for a couple of flags sticking up in the long grass, you'd never know that a golf course had been there at all. The greens had vanished and the sand traps had become hollows, filled with brambles and crabgrass. The fairways had turned to pasture, waist-high grass bending in the breeze. This had all happened, as far as I could make out, in the span of a single summer. The golf course had been left untended and nature had run riot. The famous Dylan Thomas poem "The Force That Through the Green Fuse Drives the Flower" imagines nature as a kind of unstoppable and explosive energy, so powerful it's also destructive. That's what happened at Sun Valley. It was as if a growth-bomb had gone off. So much wildness made the place seem a little scary and, though it was bursting with life, a little forlorn.

Dying

I realized, with a pang for my dear friend, that this is the other side of summer. It springs up so fast and so green, and rushes on so heedlessly, that there's no checking it, really. Sooner or later, it sweeps everything under.

Epilogue

Now that I'm more than twice as old as I was when I met Chip, I think a lot about death, which I sometimes picture as a bus—a yellow school bus, to be precise—idling around the corner, waiting to run me over. Often I wake up in the middle of the night, hearing that bus's engine, and to distract myself, I replay old golf holes in my head or recall scenes from summers past. Sailing with the kids. Bridge-jumping. Collecting fireflies on the lawn. I take imaginary walks on the beach with Nancy and the family—or, rather, with our earlier selves, younger and slimmer. I sometimes picture a whole troop of us—Nancy, our children, and their children; Chip and Gay; Steggie and his wife, Carol; Tom Winner and his wife, Anne—at the top of the big sand dune adjacent to the beach parking lot, the one from which you can see the ocean as you come up over the rise. In my mind's eye, we're stretched out in a line, one by one, like a picture in a calendar or a scene in a Bergman movie. Chip is leading the way and pauses to put on his sunglasses. A couple of the little kids are straggling and I call to them—silently, because there's no sound in this picture—to hurry up. The sun is shining. There's a breeze rustling from the southwest. There's a picnic lunch in the cooler—sandwiches and some brewskis, seltzer for the kids. Everyone has put on sunscreen. We've checked for ticks and I've got a book with me in case I get bored. There's a chance of rain in the forecast, but it probably won't come for hours.

Acknowledgments

My daughter, Sarah, had the idea for this book. She persisted in encouraging me, even when I wasn't sure I wanted to be encouraged, and at a crucial point took time from her own very busy publishing career to give me a road map showing where I needed to go. I can't thank her enough.

My wife, Nancy, has always been my first reader. In this case she was also the last, and she read the manuscript about a dozen times in between, saving me from all kinds of mistakes. She hates to be complimented, but, sorry, Nance, you need to be thanked here in public. Our son, Ben, the best writer in the family, also rescued me from countless errors of tone and judgment and at a time when he, too, was busy with a project of his own. I'm very grateful for his help. And I need to mention four other readers who painstakingly went over an early draft, suggesting scores of improvements both big and small: my old friends and colleagues Daphne Merkin and Deborah Garrison, and Roger Angell and his wife, Peggy Moorman. I'm immensely grateful to them all, especially to Roger, who, now in his second century, has been my editor and role model for fifty years.

My agent, Amanda Urban, has been putting up with me for almost as long. She is famous in the business for her forbearance as well as her shrewdness, for sticking with writers over the long haul, but surely I have tried her patience more than most. Thanks, Binky.

Ever since I was commissioned a few years ago to write a short history of Knopf, it's been my dream to be published by that legendary house. Now that I actually am a Knopf author, my admiration for the place has only increased. My heartfelt thanks to everyone there who worked on this book—my editor, Paul Bogaards; his assistants, Olivia Decker and the amazing Todd Portnowitz; Maria Massey and Lisa Silverman, my copy editors; Michael Collica, my text designer; my marketer, Matthew Sciarappa; my publicists, Gabrielle Brooks and Nicholas Latimer; and the peerless Chip Kidd, who designed the jacket. And, speaking of the jacket, I don't want to forget John Irving, who in his generosity gave me not only a blurb but also a title.

Someone else I shouldn't leave out is Edward Pitoniak. I think of him as a winter friend, but he nevertheless helped shape some of my ideas about summer.

Finally, I owe an immense debt to Chip Gillespie's widow, Gay—for years of friendship (and great meals) and for sharing so many of her memories. They both cheered me up and made me miss him even more.

A Note About the Author

Charles McGrath, known as Chip, is the former deputy editor of *The New Yorker* and a former editor of *The New York Times Book Review*. He is currently a contributing writer at *The New York Times*. He is the editor of *Golf Stories*, two Library of America volumes, and is an occasional contributor to *Golf Digest*. He lives with his wife in northern New Jersey and southeastern Massachusetts.

A Note on the Type

This book was set in Janson, a typeface named for the Dutchman Anton Janson, but which is actually the work of Nicholas Kis (1650–1702). The type is an excellent example of the influential and sturdy Dutch types that prevailed in England up to the time William Caslon (1692–1766) developed his own incomparable designs from them.

Typeset by Scribe
Philadelphia, Pennsylvania

Printed and bound by Berryville Graphics
Berryville, Virginia

Designed by Michael Collica